STUDIA PANOPOLITANA

Occasional Paper 2

Reichert Verlag Wiesbaden 2017

Petrie's 1907/08 Dig Season Near Sūhāǧ

Part I: The photographic record

Rafed El-Sayed

Reichert Verlag Wiesbaden 2017

In remembrance of Professor Yahia Salah Saber El-Masry
(23.11.1951–24.03.2013)

Bibliografische Information der Deutschen Nationalbibliothek
Die Deutsche Nationalbibliothek verzeichnet diese Publikation
in der Deutschen Nationalbibliografie; detaillierte bibliografische Daten
sind im Internet über http://dnb.dnb.de abrufbar.

Gedruckt auf säurefreiem Papier
(alterungsbeständig – pH7, neutral)

ISBN: 978-3-95490-264-4
www.reichert-verlag.de

Printed in Germany

Contents

Editor's Foreword

This occasional paper, the second in the new series *Studia Panopolitana* which is devoted to research on the ninth nome of Upper Egypt and its metropolis Aḫmīm-Panopolis, is the first to appear in book form. It is furthermore the first in a series dealing with the expedition of the British School of Archaeology in Egypt (BSAE), directed by Flinders Petrie in 1907/08, at three sites on the western escarpment of the Libyan desert plateau, in the modern Sūhāğ district and within the boundaries of the ancient ninth nome of Upper Egypt, the 'Nomós Panopolites' of the Greek sources. In his reports, Petrie, viewing the three sites as part of a contiguous historic landscape, refers to them as Hagarseh, Athribis, and the coenobium of Athribis at the White Monastery or 'Deir Amba Shenudeh'.

Petrie did not report on the results of his 1907/08 Sūhāğ-season at great length; many aspects of the work conducted remain unclear down until today. One reason is that the extant archival documents have not been easily accessible, and so could not readily be evaluated. A major purpose of this volume is to provide access and to contextualise the (for the most part) unpublished excavation photographs held in the Petrie Museum of Egyptian Archaeology, London. In this, the research follows the model set ten years ago by the first volume of *Unseen Images: Archive Photographs in the Petrie Museum: Gurob, Sedment and Tarkhan*. It is especially welcome that Ivor Pridden, co-editor of that publication, could provide his expertise to support the present volume of *Studia Panopolitana*, which may in a real sense be considered a continuation of the *Unseen Images* project. The reprocessing of the published and unpublished documentation and the finds deriving from the work of the Sūhāğ expedition also aims to clarify the spatial extent of this brief excavation season, intended only as a one-off, stop-gap measure, which resulted, amongst other things, in the distribution of diverse finds to a previously indeterminate number of destinations.

Acknowledgements

The project producing the results described here was funded, starting in 2012 and continuing through 2017, by a Dilthey Fellowship awarded me by the Volkswagen Foundation; I gratefully acknowledge this support here.

I am very much obliged to the late Professor Yahia Salah Saber El-Masry (1951–2013) who guided and supported my research on the Aḫmīm district over more than one and half decades. After having directed excavations himself for fourteen years at the site of Athribis-Atrīpe on behalf of the EAO/SCA, he encouraged me to establish a joint German-Egyptian mission for work at the site in 1998. Over nine years I had the unique opportunity to work closely with Yahia El-Masry at Athribis-Atrīpe, a privilege for which I am deepfully grateful.

My thanks are due to the Petrie Museum and Curator Alice Stevenson for the permission to work on and publish the PMA negatives for 'Athribis' and 'Hagarseh'. Special thanks go to Ivor Pridden who kindly provided high resolution scans of the negatives fulfilling other requests as well. Thanks are due to Emma Libonati who assisted me with the perusal of the archival material and provided high resolution scans of the notebooks and pocket diaries. To Pia Edquist and Tracy Golding I owe a debt for their kind assistance during my research visits to the Petrie Museum.

I am grateful to Sonja Grünert (Bochum) for drawing the vectorised plans and editing some of the photographs; to Esther Wegener (University of Göttingen) for her help with the preparation of other figures; to Konstantin Lakomy (University of Göttingen) for contributing the line drawing fig. 1; to Ken Parry and Malcolm Choat (Macquarie University, Sydney) for providing reports and photographs for the site of al-Hağārisa.

For their assistance with different concerns at the British Museum I would like to thank Samuel Atkins, Caroline Barton, George Benson, Georgi Parpulov, Virginia Smithson and Susanne Woodhouse.

To Stephen Quirke (University College London) and John Taylor (The British Museum) I am indebted for fruitful discussions of different aspects of my research and several useful suggestions. Finally I thank the anonymous copy editors for help with the English text; any remaining errors are my own.

W. M. Flinders Petrie's 1907/08 Dig Season Near Sūhāğ

Re-considering the records and relocating the finds from the BSAE excavations at the sites of al-Hağārisa, Athribis-Atrīpe, and the Shenute Monastery (ad-Dayr al-Abyaḍ)

Part I: The photographic record: Views of sites, monuments, and artefacts

By Rafed El-Sayed

This is the first in a series of planned articles on the BSAE expedition directed by Flinders Petrie in 1907/08 at three separate Upper Egyptian sites, located within three kilometres of each other on the west bank of the Nile in the Sūhāğ district. Petrie used the name 'Athribis' for all three in published and unpublished accounts of his work. The following attempted reexamination of Petrie's published reports and unpublished records was undertaken in the context of the author's field work and current research on the archaeology and topography of the region, based primarily on work conducted in museums and archives. One aim has been the localisation and identification of finds made in the vicinity of Sūhāğ published by Petrie only cursorily in his reports of 1908 and 1909. Shortly after arrival in London, the objects were distributed among several collections in the United Kingdom and continental Europe. In 2012 the author and his team began locating and recording the objects for renewed documentation and reprocessing. This contribution focuses on publication and analysis of photographs, for the most part unpublished, made during the 1907/08 season near Sūhāğ and today in the Petrie Museum Archive, London.

I Introduction

1.0 Preliminary remarks

Until today much remains unclear concerning the work conducted and the results achieved during Petrie's investigation of the sites subsumed under his use of the term Athribis. This is true concerning the published reports as well as the unpublished photographic record. Despite some remaining uncertainties, the photographs provide unique documentation of the region in 1907/08. Furthermore, they supplement our knowledge of the early twentieth century landscapes of the Sūhāğ area and document Petrie's interest in landscape photography.[1]

The ancient and modern history of archaeological sites within the borders of the historical ninth nome of Upper Egypt that includes the sites at the foot of the western mountain chain near Sūhāğ **(pl. I)**, is a focus of the author's continuing research.[2] One of its aims is the reconstruction of the sacred landscapes here – their topography, toponymy, and archaeology. The approach involves not just the geography of the area and the archaeology of the monumental sites but also the material culture recovered. The artefacts, now dispersed in collections world wide, were once embedded in the sacred landscape; thus very often their iconography makes reference to the topography with which they were originally associated.

Since Petrie did not return to the sites near Sūhāğ for further clarification, his investigations in the area remained provisional.[3] The results were published in 1908 and 1909 and most of the artefacts Petrie was allotted at the

1 On the importance of the documentation for the author's approach see R. El-Sayed, '*Die Archäologie des religiösen Wandels. Kultlandschaft und materielle Kultur des Raumes von Ahmīm-Panopolis von der Spätantike bis in das frühe Mittelalter [3.-9. Jh.]*' (in preparation).

2 For the author's habilitation project on '*The Archaeology of Religious Change*' (s. note 1) cf. the website of the Mîn-Panos project <www.min-panos.uni-goettingen.de.>

3 Before leaving for Memphis in January 1908 Petrie still considered returning to the Sūhāğ sites, cf. M. S. Drower, *Letters from the Desert: The Correspondence of Flinders and Hilda Petrie* (Oxford, 2004), 184.

division were distributed among the supporters of his work shortly after the end of the season in 1908. Since then very little attention was paid to the objects and records. It would be the early 1980s before exploration of the sites was resumed by foreign and Egyptian missions. One among them was initiated by the author in 1998 and directed jointly with Yahia El-Masry, then director of the local Sūhāğ Inspectorate for Antiquities from 2003 until 2011.[4] The reconsideration of the unpublished records and traceable finds related to the 1907/08 Sūhāğ mission began in 2010[5] and continues, since 2012, in the framework of the Göttingen Mîn-Panos project. A central goal of this project is the creation of an archaeological information system for the ninth nome of Upper Egypt.[6] The AIS comprises primary data including maps, photographs, drawings, etc. as well as archival material, along with secondary data such as excavation reports, both published and unpublished, travellogues and so forth. It will in future serve as a web-based tool for interdisciplinary research on the area.

One of the first archaeological excavations on the west bank of the Panopolite Nome was Petrie's venture of 1907/08. The focus of the following pages is the excavated sites and monuments as recorded in Petrie's publications, unpublished records, and his on-site photographs which are currently among the archival material in the Petrie Museum, London. Sections 1.1 to 1.3 reconsider the 1907/08 season and the problem of identifying the sites, monuments, and artefacts pictured in the photographs. Part II is an annotated catalogue of the Petrie Museum Archive negatives (PMAN), not presented in numerical order, but arranged according to the sites and monuments identified in the photographs. To introduce each site a short bibliography and a brief general description is provided. Preliminary conclusions and appendices – a list of negative numbers, a set of thumbnail images, and plates with addtional illustrations – are provided.

1.1 Petrie's dig season near Sūhāğ: duration, team, work assignments and objectives

Petrie's final excavation report is rather uninformative as far as the precise length of the season, the staff involved, and their responsibilities:[7]

> *We accordingly camped there* [scil. at Athribis], *while some of the party were two miles further north, at the Deir Amba Shenudeh, or White Monastery, and our work extended to copying tombs two miles to the south, near Hagarseh.* [...] *meanwhile, we have done in a month or two as much as a temporary excavation will allow. 3. The party at Athribis fluctuated in number, owing to work elsewhere. Mr. Ernest Mackay* [8] *was there for ten weeks, from the beginning to the end of the work. I was there for seven weeks, arranging the work and copying. Herr Schuler of Munich was occupied in copying for a month, mainly on the zodiac tomb. Mr. Wainwright* [9] *was copying for three weeks. Mr. E. Ward* [10]*, Mr. Ivo Gregg, and Mr. Humphry Hill were at the place for a fortnight, but mostly concerned with finishing the plan of the Coenobium, which they had excavated during a fortnight before. Mr. Gregory Wyatt stayed for ten days, and did some of the copying. The net amount of work in excavating and copying at Athribis was about six weeks to two months for three people.*

Additional information concerning the duration of the season and the work accomplished is given by Petrie in his authobiography:[11]

4 R. El-Sayed and Y. El-Masry (eds), *Athribis I: General Site Survey 2003 – 2007. Archaeological & Conservation Studies. The Gate of Ptolemy IX. Architecture and Inscriptions* (Le Caire, 2012). For the history of research in the area, see 1.2, below. A comprehensive review covering the 17th to the 21st century will be included in the author's habilitation (see n. 1).

5 El-Sayed, in El-Sayed and El-Masry (eds), *Athribis* I, 77 and 77 n. 28–30.

6 See R. El-Sayed, C. Häuber and F. X. Schütz, *'AIS Mîn-Panos': Developing an Archaeological Information System for the Panopolite Nome (Akhmîm) in Upper Egypt* (Studia Panopolitana, Occasional Paper 1; Göttingen, 2016) <webdoc.sub.gwdg.de/pub/mon/2016/1-el-sayed.pdf>.

7 W. M. Fl. Petrie, *Athribis* (BSAE 14; London, 1908), 1–2. Author's remarks and numbers of footnotes in [].

8 On Mackay see M. L. Bierbrier, *Who Was Who in Egyptology* (4th rev. edn; London, 2012), 348.

9 On G. A. Wainwright, see Bierbrier, *Who Was Who*, 562.

10 On Ward see A. Stephenson, 'Artefacts of Excavation', *EA* 46 (2015), 29. To date it has not been possible to locate information about other members of Petrie's team.

11 W. M. Fl. Petrie, *Seventy Years in Archaeology* (London, 1930), 209–210.

On November 14, 1907, I started, the students being Mackay and Ward as last year, also Gregg and Hill, and Schuler, a German architect sent by von Bissing. We began by settling at Deir el Abyad, December 2nd, in order to find the meaning of ruins near the monastery. [...] *After a week I moved to Athribis, and a week later our party settled there. The temple proved to be entirely Ptolemaic, and to have the peculiar feature of a peristyle court surrounding the whole, probably to Greek influence. I copied much of the sculpture,* [...] *We copied the very rare examples of zodiac horoscopes of Roman age, painted on tomb ceilings. Some rock tombs of the IVth or Vth century at Hagarseh were also fully copied and published. On January 1, Ward and Schuler went to Memphis to begin building our house; but German ideas did not fit with Egyptian conditions, and there was hardly a habitable room by the 27th when I moved there.*

More precise information can be found in the pocket diary concerning the years 1907–08.[12] The respective entries read as follows [**pl. II**]: 30th of November 1907: "*Up to Sohag with Schuler*",[13] 1st of December 1907: "*Over to Deir Abyad.* [?] *Athribis*",[14] 25th January 1908: "*Corniche found to be reused in floor, 1st temple destroyed*", 26th January 1908: "*packing*", 27th January 1908: "*Down to Bedreshen – 3 rooms built, all soaking wet"*. Thus the field work at the Sūhāǧ sites commensed on December 2, 1907 and continued until January 25th 1908.[15]

Petrie explained his motives for excavating the sites near Sūhāǧ and outlined the main objectives he pursued as follows:[16]

To work Memphis the season should be as late as possible, for the subsidence of the water. Hence it was necessary to fill the earlier part of the season by short work further south. A ruined temple was known at Athribis near Sohag, so I applied for that region, and also to work Memphis.

The same motivation for working the sites is given in the introduction to the excavation report:[17]

Before beginning work at Memphis, two or three months can only be spent on excavation in drier sites, for the inundation covers the area of the great temple of Ptah till the middle of February, and the surrounding mounds are so damp below, and so miry with continual rain, that work on them is not desirable in December and January. In view of this, the work of the British School was resumed in Upper Egypt, in the same region as last year,[18] *for the beginning of the season.*

Petrie might have considered working at the Sūhāǧ sites as early as 1901, when he first visited the area during a return trip from Abydos (see below).[19] Already during his first short visit to the region that year, he had copied some inscriptions at Athribis-Atrīpe.[20] On the peculiarities of the site Petrie stated:[21]

Seven years ago I had noticed, near Sohag, the site known as Athribis; here there appeared to be the ruins of a temple, covered by sand, on the desert edge. It is so seldom that temple ruins are on the desert, and not swallowed in the growth of Nile deposits in the plain, that it seemed desirable to examine this.

12 On the pocket diaries see P. Del Vesco, 'Day after day with Flinders Petrie. Pocket diaries from the archive of the Petrie Museum of Egyptian Archaeology, University College London', in M. Betrò and G. Miniaci (eds), *Talking along the Nile: Ippolito Rossellini, travellers and scholars of the 19th century in Egypt. Proceedings of the international conference held on the occasion of the presentation of progetto Rosellini. Pisa, June 14–16, 2012*, (Pisa, 2013). A digital copy of the diaries was kindly provided to the author by the Petrie Museum.

13 Page 109, see **pl. II**.

14 Page 110, see **pl. II**.

15 In W. M. Fl. Petrie, *Memphis* I, (BSAE 14; London, 1909), 1 January 26 is the date cited for Petrie's arrival at Memphis. *Pace* El-Sayed and El-Masry, *Athribis* I, 57.

16 Petrie, *Seventy Years*, 209.

17 Petrie, *Athribis*, 1. See also, British School of Archaeology in Egypt, *Catalogue of Egyptian Antiquities, found by Prof. Flinders Petrie and Students at Memphis and Athribis. 1908. Exhibited at University College, Gower St., London, W.C., June 29th to July 25th* (London, 1908), 3.

18 During the season 1906/07 Petrie had worked at Abydos, 50 kilometres south of Sūhāǧ.

19 M. S. Drower, *Flinders Petrie: A Life in Archaeology* (London, 1985), 263, 308. Drower, *Letters from the Desert*, 165.

20 Drower, *Flinders Petrie*, 263. This copying most probably took place in the 'zodiac tomb', which was presumably accessible on Petrie's first visit; see Petrie, *Athribis*, 12: '*For many years a tomb has stood open,* [...].'

21 Petrie, *Athribis*, 1.

1.2 The results of the BSAE excavations: published reports etc., unpublished records and artefacts in museums

The final results of the 1907/08 Sūhāğ season were presented in '*Athribis*',[22] the first of two excavation reports of that year. A short *addendum* was provided in the second report of the 14th BSAE memoir year, '*Memphis* I'.[23] Some further notes are retrievable from two occasional publications of the same year – a brief descriptive catalogue for an exhibition on the 1908 season, organised by Petrie and his students, shown at University College,[24] and a short announcement published by the British School concerning the work accomplished during 1908.[25]

The excavation report related to the work in Upper Egypt combines the results achieved at all three sites near Sūhāğ: 'Hagarseh' [**pl. III**], Athribis-Atrīpe [**pl. IVb**], and the Shenute Monastery [**pl. IVa**]. In general, the work centred on epigraphic and architectural recording – drawings, photographs, and descriptions of the epigraphic and architectural record. Most of the pencil drawings were inked on site so that the plates were ready for publication before Petrie returned to London.[26] Tracings of the pottery and drawings of the small finds were only done in London.[27]

As was customary, the final publication included only a selection of the photographs taken on site.[28] Forty-eight of the photographs Petrie took in the course of his excavations have been identified in the archives of the Petrie Museum of Egyptian Archaeology, University College London.[29] Many of the glass negatives bear notations that aid in ascribing them to specific sites.[30] In the case of the 'Athribis' negatives, fifteen of fourty-eight are annotated. Aside from the glass negatives and Petrie's publications, the notebooks and pocket diaries[31] are the only additional records known to exist today for the years 1907 and 1908.[32] The last are most problematic, not only due to illegibility, but mainly because, in general, there is no discernible structure enabling identification of the precise find spot of a particular item. The notebooks provide little information concerning the discoveries of the season that go beyond the published excavation report. On the other hand, some scattered remarks about the 1907/08 season near Sūhāğ can be also gleaned from Petrie's correspondence.[33]

The artefacts that were excavated and sent to London in spring 1908 still can add fundamentally to our undersatanding of the sites investigated.[34] Most were distributed in summer 1908, primarily among British and continental European collections. Only some remained at University College London and are at the Petrie Museum today. The artefacts, embedded in multiple excavation and museum contexts, will be discussed in detail in the forthcoming segments of the study.

---

22 Petrie, *Athribis*.

23 Petrie, *Memphis* I.

24 British School of Archaeology in Egypt, *Catalogue 1908*. On the post season exhibitions see now A. Thornton, 'Exhibition Season: Annual Archaeological Exhibitions in London, 1880s-1930s', *Bulletin of the History of Archaeology* 25,2 (2015), 1–18. See also A. Thornton, ''... a certain faculty for extracting cash': Collective Sponsorship in Late 19th and Early 20th Century British Archaeology', *Present Pasts* 5,1 (2013), 1–12.

25 The British School of Archaeology in Egypt, *Excavations at Memphis. 1908* (London, 1908).

26 Drower, *Letters from the Desert*, 182–183.

27 Petrie, *Memphis* I, 15. On the pottery cf. the forthcoming second segment of this study. On the small finds see the third segment of this study.

28 M. Serpico, 'History of the Petrie Photographic Archive', in J. Picton and I. Pridden (eds), *Unseen Images: Archive Photographs in the Petrie Museum. Volume I: Gurob, Sedment and Tarkhan* (London, 2008), 10. On page 28 of the 1907 notebook Petrie lists the illustrations to be included into the final publication.

29 See below 1.2.

30 On these annotations see Serpico, in Picton and Pridden (eds), *Unseen Images*, 10.

31 Discussion of this recently digitised record is found in Del Vesco, in Betrò and Miniaci (eds), *Talking along the* Nile, 83–92.

32 Originals of the diaries and copies of the journals were consulted at the Petrie Museum.

33 Drower, *Letters from the Desert*, 165, 182–184. The copies of the 1907 and 1908 journals hold at the Petrie Museum did not include any letters concerning the Sūhāğ mission. At Manchester, however, a copy of Petrie's letter concerning this mission dating to January 1st, 1908 could be identified. The letter does, however, not provide any information going beyond the published reports.

34 In the Egyptian Museum, Cairo, no finds could be located that could be attributed with certainty to Petrie's 1907/08 campaign at the sites near Sūhāğ.

1.3 Identifying sites, monuments and artefacts in the records

For various reasons Petrie's 1907/08 dig season presents problems of interpretation. Confusion arises, first of all, with the attribution of finds either to Memphis or to one of the Sūhāǧ sites since both missions, one in northern and the other in southern Egypt, took place during the same season. The finds arrived together in London in spring 1908; some mix-up might even have occured during the packing as well as during the unpacking of them. Furthermore, for published and archival provenance information, even museum register entries and words or numbers written directly on objects, the same critical assessment has to be applied as to any historical document.[35]

The main potential for confusion, however, arises from the topography and related material culture of the two sites located at the mountain of Atrīpe (**pl. I**), since both were closely associated with the toponym (geonym) Athribis-Atrīpe (see below).[36] These two sites, three kilometres apart, were in fact closely related, at least during late antiquity (ca. 280–850 AD; see below). They must, however, be clearly differentiated topographically and from an archaeological standpoint as well.

Before late antiquity these sites, although within the same cultic landscape, were independent settlements. Early in the fourth century AD they both became associated with the 'White Monastery federation'. Centred at the northern extension of Mount Atrīpe, this federation also comprised the monastic site known today as 'Pshoi Monastery' (Dayr al-Anbā Bīšūy) or 'Red Monastery' (ad-Dayr al-Aḥmar) respectively.[37] The third site, the necropolis of al-Haǧārisa, is located three kilometres south of Athribis-Atrīpe. It was tentatively identified by Petrie as the cemetery of the predecessor settlement of 'Athribis' which he presumed was located at the modern village of aṣ-Ṣalʿā'.[38] He based his hypothesis on the fact that he could not locate any evidence for occupation earlier than the Late Period at Athribis-Atrīpe, even though at the site of al-Haǧārisa, the tombs dated as early as the Old Kingdom. While this is not the place to go into the details of this problem it should be mentioned that the attribution of al-Haǧārisa to the ninth nome of Upper Egypt is not entirely certain.[39] Futhermore, the cemetery belonged to a town named *Ḥr-šn*,[40] which must be distinguished from Athribis-Atrīpe. This renders Petrie's hypothesis quite unlikely.[41]

Today all three sites are located within the borders of the administrative district of Sūhāǧ. The modern town of Sūhāǧ[42] is situated on the west bank of the Nile, directly on the river and thus about six kilometres distant from the western mountains and both the Shenute Monastery and Athribis-Atrīpe. It must not be amalgamated with the monastic sites on the desert fringe, as has sometimes been the case.[43] In this study the following nomenclature is employed. The place name Athribis(-Atrīpe), if not set off typographically (e.g., with quotation marks), refers to the archaeological site of Athribis (Atrībīs in modern Arabic) situated near the village of Naǧʿ aš-Šayḫ Ḥamad. To distinguish between the archaeological site named after the village of al-Haǧārisa and the village itself, the former is always specified as *site/necropolis* of al-Haǧārisa, while the latter is called the *village* of al-Haǧārisa. The White Monastery (of Shenute) is so named, without adding 'at Atrīpe' or a similar qualifier.

35 See the next part of this study. I thank Stephen Quirke for discussing this aspect with me.

36 R. El-Sayed, 'Schenute und die Tempel von Atripe. Zur Umnutzung des Triphisbezirks in der Sptantike', in H. Knuf et al. (eds), *Honi soit qui mal y pense. Studien zum pharaonischen, griechisch-römischen und spätantiken Ägypten zu Ehren von Heinz-Josef Thissen*, (OLA 194; Leuven etc 2010), 519–538, pls. 93–97. El-Sayed, in El-Sayed and El-Masry (eds), *Athribis* I, 7.

37 B. Layton, *The Canons of Our Fathers: Monastic Rules of Shenoute*, (Oxford, 2014), 11–14.

38 Petrie, *Athribis*, 1. The identification goes back to C. R. Lepsius (see below).

39 N. Kanawati, *El-Hagarsa* I, (ACE Reports 4; Sydney, 1993), 7 considers it more likely that the necropolis and the associated town were situated within the borders of the 9th nome. See as well N. Kanawati, 'Akhmim', in K. A. Bard (ed.), *Encyclopedia of the Archaeology of Ancient Egypt* (London and New York, 1999) 125–126 and H. Brunner, *Die Anlagen der ägyptischen Felsgräber bis zum Mittleren Reich* (*ÄF* 3; Glückstadt-Hamburg-New York, 1936), 23.

40 El-Sayed and El-Masry (eds), *Athribis* I, 15.

41 Discussed in detail in El-Sayed, *Die Archäologie des religiösen Wandels* (forthcoming).

42 For the available information on the archaeology and history of the town site of Sūhāǧ see El-Sayed, in El-Sayed and El-Masry (eds), *Athribis* I, 5, 9. The subject is dealt with more extensively in the author's forthcoming study on the Aḫmīm district.

43 Verbeek, s.v. 'Sohag', in *LÄ* IV, 1052–1054; D. Klotz, 'Two Studies on the Late Period Temples at Abydos', *BIFAO* 110 (2010), 129; S. Grallert, *Bauen – Stiften – Weihen. Ägyptische Bau- und Restaurierungsinschriften von den Anfängen bis zur 30. Dynastie*, (ADAIK 18; Berlin, 2001), 490.

1.4 Locating and contextualising the finds

For localising the finds reproduced or only mentioned in the publications, a systematic procedure was not practicable since no comprehensive register of them exists. Neither the notebooks[44] nor the distribution lists[45] include such information. According to a few indications in Petrie's publications and the information that can be extracted from the distribution lists, objects were sent in the main to the following museums and private sponsors (who very often sold them to museums or other collectors):[46] London, The British Museum; London, Victoria and Albert Museum; Bristol, The Bristol Museum; Manchester, The Manchester Museum; Edinburgh, Royal Scottish Museum (now the National Museum of Scotland); Brussels, Musée du Cinquantenaire; Munich, collection von Bissing, now in large part in the Allard Pierson Museum, Amsterdam.[47]

The contextualisation of the finds is, again, a complex affair which will be discussed in more detail in forthcoming installments of the study. For the majority of finds attribution to any one of the three different sites – Athribis-Atrīpe, al-Haǧārisa site, Shenute Monastery site – remains in general uncertain. Moreover, in some instances, a possible attribution to Memphis must even be considered (see below).

II Petrie Museum Archive negatives: Sites and monuments in the photographic record

2.1 'Athribis' in the Petrie Museum Archives (PMA)

Forty-eight[48] negatives in the Petrie Museum archives are currently ascribed to the 1907/08 season near Sūhāǧ, although for some attributions doubts persist. More may exist among the unidentified negatives while others might have been lost.[49] Views of the landscape, monuments, and finds at/from the sites of al-Haǧārisa and Athribis-Atrīpe (near Naǧʿ aš-Šayḫ Ḥamad) are included, but no photographs of the Shenute Monastery site could be identified and probably none were ever taken during the BSAE excavations at this site.[50] Petrie himself took most of the photographs.[51] Those of the tomb of Mery II in the cemetery of al-Haǧārisa were, however, reportedly taken by Ernest Mackay.[52] Unfortunately, no photograph of the exhibition held following the season could be identified among the PMA negatives.

44 On the notebooks see S. Quirke, 'Petrie Archives in London and Oxford', in: D. Magee et al (eds), *Sitting Besides Lepsius. Studies in Honour of Jaromir Malek at the Griffith Institute* (OLA 185; Leuven-Paris-Walpole, Mass, 2009), 442–461.

45 For the distribution system see A. Stevenson, 'Artefacts of Excavation. The British collection and distribution of Egyptian finds to museums', 1880–1915, *JHC* 26,1 (2013), 89–102.

46 See the list on the 'Digital Egypt for Universities' website <http://www.ucl.ac.uk/museums-static/digitalegypt//archaeology/athribismemphisdistribution.html > and PM V, 33 and now the website <www.egyptartefacts.griffith.ox.ac.uk>.

47 On the history of von Bissing's collection see C. E. Loeben, *Die Ägypten-Sammlung des Museum August Kestner und ihre Kriegsverluste*, (Rahden/Westf. 2011), 85–115; A. Grimm, S. Schoske, *Friedrich Wilhelm Freiherr von Bissing. Ägyptologe – Mäzen – Sammler*, (Ramses 5; München, 2010).

48 This is the total number in the PMA ascribed to 'Athribis' and 'Hagarseh'. The current labelling of the negatives was done in the 1980's by Joan Merritt. Cf. Quirke, 'Petrie Archives' in: Magee et al (eds), *Fs Malek*, 442. The unpublished inventory *Petrie Museum of Egyptian Archaeology University College London, Photographic Archive* I: *Negatives from Archaeological Sites* (London, 1996) compiled by Merritt lists 46 negatives for Athribis (without 'Hagarseh') but still including one view (PMAN 625) that has without any doubt to be attributed to the site of al-Haǧārisa.

49 The history of the archives is told by Serpico, in Picton and Pridden (eds), *Unseen Images*, 10 and in more detail by Quirke, 'Petrie Archives', in Magee et al (eds), *Fs Malek*, 442; idem, 'Borderlines: questions of definition among the documentary and pictorial archives amid the collections of the Petrie Museum', Egyptian & Egyptological Documents, Archives, Libraries I (Milano, 2009), 129–130. A systematic revision of the archives by the author proved impractical. On the history of the Petrie Museum see now A. Stevenson and D. Challis, 'Introduction: a modest little museum' in A. Stevenson (ed.), The Petrie Museum of Egyptian Archaeology. Characters and collections (London, 2015) 11–23.

50 There is no explicit mention of photographs being taken at the Shenute monastery site.

51 This can be assumed based on the explicit mention of photographs taken by other members of the mission, see Petrie, *Athribis*, 4.

52 Petrie, *Athribis*, 4.

2.2 'Hagarseh' (al-Haǧārisa, site)

El-Sayed & El-Masry, *Athribis* I (2012), 15, 53–55, 57–58. – Grallert, *Bauen* (2001), 490. – Bard, *Encyclopedia*, 124–128, 316–319 (1999). – Kanawati, *El-Hagarsa* I–III (1993–1995). – Schenkel, *MHT* (1965), 38–40. – PM V, 34–35 (1937). – Brunner, *Felsgräber* (1936), 23–25, 61–62, 79, 86. – Urk. I, 266–267 (1933). – Petrie, *Athribis* (1908), 2–4, pls. I–XIII. – *LD*, Text II, 159–160.

2.2.1 The Site: location,[53] toponymy, topography, and history of exploration

The archaeological site of al-Haǧārisa is located at 26°29'20''N/31°40'05''E; it covers an area of low desert and extends to the escarpment of the Libyan Desert plateau. The site was named by Petrie after the modern village of al-Haǧārisa[54] [26°28'30''N/31°40'30''E], half a kilomtre to the southeast of the escarpment. The nearest village of noteworthy size at that time was aṣ-Ṣalʿā'[55] [26°29'34''N/31°43'28''E], situated at a distance of five kilometres to the east of the archaeological site. Immediately south of al-Haǧārisa is the village of al-Kawāmil[56] (baḥrī) [26°28'05''N/31°40'56''E], that had already received mention in Lepsius' account (see below).

The archaeological site comprises a series of rock-cut tombs datable to the end of the Old Kingdom[57] and settlement remains on the low desert. At least some of the tombs were allegedly reused in later periods of Egyptian history as burial places for crocodiles.[58] Both sites were occupied in late antiquity by a monastic community recently identified as the Monastery of Apa Paulos (see below).

The first survey of the site was made by the Prussian expedition in 1845.[59] Lepsius reported extensive mounds below the tombs of al-Haǧārisa, more precisely at the village of 'kauámi',[60] a name most likely linked linguistically to al-Kawāmil baḥrī. The next expedition to al-Haǧārisa was led by Petrie, who, astonishingly, does not mention any mounds near the site.[61] Petrie's brief account of his initial brief visit in February 1901 reads:

> [...] *so we took our way to Kawamil, a straggly village on the desert edge, where men were weaving in the side alleys. While Ali had the camel unloaded and tent pitched, F. and I went off exploring to the cliff-face of the high gebel which here projects to the cultivation, and discovered a ruined Coptic monastery under the precipitous headland which was itself the home of many other brethren formerly, as all the natural caves and all the rock-cut Egyptian tombs had been used by Coptic hermits and monastics. The face of the rock was riddled with rows of small square openings, the tomb-doorways being hewn out with a lintel above: there were thirty or more in each row! We climbed up about 250 ft. to the tomb, and just got down by sunset.* [...]

This epitome can be compared to Petrie's general description of the location and condition of the site's main features in his 1908 report:[62]

> [...] *The site of the older* [scil. compared to Athribis] *city was probably more to the south, most likely at Es Sala'a, as the tombs of the Old Kingdom are opposite to that. From Sohag is seen a great headland of cliff projecting into the Nile*

53 Coordinates are given according to Esri ArcGIS online.

54 Petrie, *Athribis*, 1. M. Ramzī, *al-Qāmūs al-ǧuġrāfī li-l-bilād al-miṣrīya min ʿahd qudamāʾ al-miṣrīyīn ʾilā sanat 1945*, 3 vols. (al-Qāhira, 1953–1968), 131. Al-Haǧārisa is classified as nāḥiya/village by A. Boinet Bey, *Dictionnaire Géographique de l'Égypte* (Le Caire, 1899), 225, with 841 inhabitants in 1899.

55 Ramzī, *Qāmūs*, 123. aṣ-Ṣalʿāʾ is classified as nāḥiya/village by Boinet Bey, *Dictionnaire Géographique*, 476, with 2.926 inhabitants in 1899.

56 *LD*, Text II, 160–161. On al-Kawāmil baḥrī see Ramzī, *Qāmūs*, 131. al-Kawāmil baḥrī is classified as nāḥiya/village by Boinet Bey, *Dictionnaire Géographique*, 315, with 3.676 (including suburbs: 6.282) inhabitants in 1899.

57 Kanawati, in Bard (ed.), *Encyclopedia*, 125.

58 Petrie, *Athribis*, 3.

59 25. May 1845, *LD*, Text II, 160.

60 *LD*, Text II, 159–160; cf. El-Sayed and El-Masry, *Athribis* I, 15, 53.

61 Petrie, *Athribis*, 2 mentions only the '*brick-built deir*' in the plain. The mounds noted by Lepsius might have been located a little more to the south and were thus not recognised by Petrie. Nor is there any mention of them in his letter of 1901, see Drower, *Letters from the Desert*, 165. By 1901, Lepsius's mounds at al-Kawāmi(l), might have been dug away by *sabbāḥīn*. For *sibāḥ* exploitation in the 19th and 20th centuries cf. D. M. Bailey, 'Sebakh, Sherds and Survey', *JEA* 85 (1999), 211–218.

62 Petrie, *Athribis*, 1–2.

valley; the early tombs [scil. those of al-Haǧārisa] *are south-ward of that, and the later town* [scil. 'Athribis'] *to the north. The modern village nearest to the tombs is Hagarseh, a mile south-east* [scil. from the rock cemetery at al-Haǧārisa], *and they are here named from that place.*

[...] *Nearly five miles south of Sohag, the cliffs of the western desert are pierced with a large group of rock-tombs, as shown in the diagram-view, Pl. I.* [...] *Few of the tombs contain any inscriptions or sculpture. Most of them are small recesses, about three feet square, leading to a pit; some of them have a chamber about five feet wide above the pit. Most of them have been occupied by Coptic recluses, belonging to a brick-built deir which stands on the plain below. Some Coptic paintings remain in the chamber at the south end of the top row, and there is one scene of the ascent of Elijah.*

In the late 1980s the rock-cut tombs were reinvestigated completely for the first time by a team from Macquarie University directed by Naguib Kanawati. The architectural and epigraphic record of the decorated tombs was published shortly thereafter.[63] In 2010/11 another team from Macquarie University surveyed the Late Antique monastic remains at the site which, thanks to a Coptic inscription, could be identified as the hitherto unknown Monastery of Apa Paulos.[64]

2.2.2 Reprography of recordings

Some of the plates prepared for the publication showing inked plans and drawings were photographed by Petrie. The Petrie Museum Archive preserves photographs of five of the forty-three plates published. The photographs were probably taken for teaching purposes.[65] Some of the drawings and plans shown at the post-season exhibition held at University College were most likely the original plates.[66] With two exceptions (PMAN 591 and 592), the reprographies of published plans and tracings are neither reproduced nor commented upon here but for the sake of completeness they are included in the appended negative and thumbnail lists.

2.2.3 Site views

Among the photographs taken during the season are several general views of sites and landscapes. They must be regarded as unique documentations of the individual sites and the area of Sūhāğ-Aḫmīm which, down until the second half of the 20th century, were counted among the remote areas of Egypt, neither frequently photographed nor sketched by archaeologists, artists, or the military like other regions of Egypt.[67] PMAN 625 and 627 in particular illustrate the documentary value of the site views as regards the archaeology of each site. PMAN 622 and again 627 moreover constitute invaluable documentation of the state and development of landscapes in the Sūhāğ district in the early 20th century.

PMAN 625: This view was taken from a position up the mountain looking southeastwards. The juxtaposition of low desert at the foot of the mountain and the cultivated plain is clearly distinguishable. The view with building remains in the centre was obviously meant to show their position on the low desert ground. The structure can be identified as the '*brick-built deir*' that Petrie mentions in his excavation report.[68] The photograph shows the masonry still preserved at places nearly to the top of a second storey. The southern walls are pierced by rows of windows. Since Petrie's day the building has severely deteriorated **(see Pl. IIIb)**.[69] Its precise function remains unknown. A considerable number of circular pits dug into the soil are clearly distinguishable, distributed regularly around the structure.

63 Kanawati, *El-Hagarsa* I–III.

64 M. Choat and K. Parry, The Sohag Survey Project's unpublished internal reports for the 2010 spring and winter seasons.

65 Cf. Serpico, in Picton and Pridden (eds), *Unsean Images*, 10.

66 British School of Archaeology in Egypt, *Catalogue 1908*, 4, 5.

67 No photographs were taken e.g. by Wreszinski, cf. W. Wreszinski, *Bericht über die photographische Expedition von Kairo bis Wadi Halfa zwecks Abschluß der Materialsammlung für meinen Atlas zur altägyptischen Kulturgeschichte*, (Schriften der Königsberger Gelehrten Gesellschaft, Geisteswissenschaftliche Klasse, Jahr 4, Heft 2; Halle a. S., 1927).

68 Petrie, *Athribis*, 2.

69 M. Choat and K. Parry, The Sohag Survey Project's unpublished internal reports for the 2010 spring and winter seasons.

PMAN 625
al-Hağārisa, site. View of the 'brick-built deir' and surroundings in the low desert taken from the top of the mountain, looking southeast, no notations on negative.

PMAN 1025
al-Hağārisa, site, rock-cut tombs. General view of the site seen from a position in the low desert, looking west, notation reading 'ATHRIBIS I'.

These pits, still extant today, were obviously laid out according to a grid laid over the ruins; presumably they are evidence of test trenches dug by Petrie's workmen.[70] No mention of them is, however, made in Petrie's report of archaeological activity on the plain.[71] The empty wasteland to the southeast between the monastery and the village of al-Hağārisa, hardly recognisable in the upper right hand corner, is today entirely developed. PMAN 625 is thus a valuable record of the site's appearance in 1907/08, which has altered considerably in the interim.

PMAN 1025: The photograph was taken from a position in the midst of the low desert ground and shows a general view of the tombs cut into the cliff. The entrances are clearly visible. This photograph obviously served as the basis for Petrie's drawing of a 'diagram-view' indicating the tomb entrances reproduced on Pl. I in his excavation report, as noted on the negative. For a recent view of the site see **Pl. IIIa**.

2.2.4 Monuments

At the site of al-Hağārisa Petrie recorded four inscribed tombs in detail.[72] Only in the tomb of Mery II were photographs taken, since it alone was in condition suitably cleared for photography.[73] Aside from the '*diagram-view*' published on Pl. I and the plans and sections of the four tombs, no remains of buildings were recorded in detail.

PMAN 1027: Ernest Mackay took this photograph[74] showing the north wall of the chapel in the tomb of the Royal Chamberlain Mery.[75] During the re-recording of the tomb in the late 1980s this wall was found in a considerably deteriorated condition[76] which makes the image an important record of this monument.

As on the other two photographs, traces of the chamber's reuse in late antiquity as a monk's cell are clearly visible. In addition to a deep, nearly square niche in the centre, several circular cavities are visible on the wall. They were probably intended to secure features of the furnishings (possibly poles) in the monk's cell.[77]

PMAN 1028: Mackay was again responsible for the photograph[78] which shows the west wall of the chapel in the tomb of the Royal Chamberlain Mery.[79] It was included on Pl. XI of the excavation report.[80] The northern half of the wall surface has been entirely cut out, most probably in late antiquity, to provide a huge niche. The wall was recorded again in the early 1990s after restoration had been carried out. [81]

70 They cannot therefore be interpreted as traces of modern looting as one might infer.

71 In a letter of 22 January 1908 Petrie mentioned that Gerald Wainwright accompanied him on one of his last visits to the al-Hağārisa tombs '[...] *to ransack around, and look at all likely places for me.*' (see Drower, *Letters from the desert*, 184). If during this or comparable activities the '*brick built deir*' was examined must remain mere speculation.

72 Petrie, *Athribis*, 2.

73 Petrie, *Athribis*, 4.

74 Petrie, *Athribis*, 4.

75 A short description of the tomb and the scenes is found in Petrie, *Athribis*, 4. The drawing is reproduced in Petrie, *Athribis*, pl. X. For a more comprehensive documentation and evaluation see now Kanawati, *El-Hagarsa* I, 55–65, pls. 11–15, 41–46.

76 Kanawati, *El-Hagarsa* I, 62.

77 The furnishings might have included looms. On looms in rock cut tombs, cf. J. Sigl, 'Weaving Copts in the north tombs of Tell el-Amarna', *SAK* 40 (2011), 357–386.

78 Petrie, *Athribis*, 4.

79 Petrie, *Athribis*, 4, pl. X. Kanawati, *El-Hagarsa* I, 61, pls. 44–45.

80 Petrie, *Athribis*, pl. XII.

81 Kanawati, *El-Hagarsa* I, pl. 13–14.

PMAN 1027
al-Hağārisa, rock-cut tombs of the Old Kingdom. 'Tomb of Mery II. N. Wall.', notation reading 'ATH. X'.

PMAN 1028
al-Hağārisa, rock-cut tombs. 'Tomb of Mery II. W. Wall.' = Petrie, Athribis, pl. XI, notation reading 'ATH. XI'.

PMAN 1029
al-Hağārisa, rock-cut tombs. 'Tomb of Mery II. S. Wall.' = Petrie, Athribis, pl. XII, notation reading 'ATH. XII'.

PMAN 1029: The photograph, taken by E. Mackay,[82] of the south wall of the tomb chapel[83] is illustrated on Pl. XII of the excavation report.[84] There are several niches and post-holes distributed over the wall – nowadays they are no longer visible, following restoration work in the 1980s.[85]

2.3 Athribis-Atrīpe (Nağʿ aš-Šayḫ Ḥamad)

El-Sayed & El-Masry, *Athribis* I (2012). – Leitz, Mendel & El-Masry, *Athribis* II (2010). – El-Masry, *MDAIK* 57 (2001). – Farag et al., *MDAIK* 41 (1985), 1–8. – Petrie, *Athribis* (1908). – *LD*, *Text* II, 159–161.

2.3.1 The Site[86]: location, toponymy, topography, and history of exploration

The exact location of the Upper Egyptian monumental site known as Athribis (contemporary Arabic: Atrībīs)[87] is 26°30'10''^{N}/31°40'09''^{E}.[88] Today, the nearest settlement is the hamlet of Šayḫ Silīm, a satellite of the village of Nağʿ aš-Šayḫ Ḥamad[89] [26°30'55''^{N}/31°39'53''^{E}], that developed haphazardly, beginning not earlier than the mid-20th century, around the sheikh's tomb. In 1906 Nağʿ aš-Šayḫ Ḥamad was the inhabited settlement closest to the archaeological site as is clearly documented in PMAN 627 (see below). The village of Wannīna[90] (aš-šarqīya) [26°31'31''^{N}/31°41'01''^{E}] after which PM names the site,[91] is located about half a kilometre to the east of the archaeological site comprising the ancient mound on the low desert at the foot of the cliff and a necropolis of rock-cut tombs extending over a distance of more than 1.7 kilometres in the escarpment of the Libyan desert.[92]

The toponymy of the site and the surrounding area is complex, due to linguistic misinterpretations and toponymic interferences stretching far back into both the history of the region itself and of modern research.[93] The actual site of Athribis-Atrīpe is situated at the foot of the promontory known since late antiquity as 'Mount Atrīpe' (Coptic: ⲡⲧⲟⲟⲩⲛⲁⲧⲣⲓⲡⲉ, Arabic: Ğabal Adrība). While the name 'Athribis' pertaining to the site near Sūhāğ is ahistoric and gave cause initially for much confusion with the homonymous city of the Delta (*Ḥw.t-ḥrj-jb*),[94] the Coptic name 'Atrīpe' goes back to *Ḥw.t-Rpy.t*, 'Sanctuary of the goddes Repyt'. This sanctuary was most probably since the Middle Kingdom at the latest located at the site of Upper Egyptian Athribis. In late Ptolemaic times it became one of the largest temple sites within the ninth nome of Upper Egypt. Its fame, however, originated from its association with the famous abbot Shenute 'of Atrīpe', more precisely 'of Mount Atrīpe'. Shenute received this epithet not from the village of Atrīpe but from the mountainious region to which he had retreated early in his career. The geonym 'Atrīpe' referring to the 'sanctuary of the goddess Repit' (Demotic: *Ḥw.t-tꜣ-Rpy.t*) denoted the mountainous region stretching from the valley (see below PMAN 626) north of the rock-cut tombs at al-Hağārisa to the valley south of the site of the Shenute (White) Monastery.

The extensive necropolis of rock-cut tombs in the western cliff includes vast quarry areas and a rock-cut temple; a quarter of the roughly rectangular-shaped mound immediately below the cliff is occupied by a precinct with two temples. The remainder of the mound includes the domestic and industrial quarters of the ancient town. Most

82 Petrie, *Athribis*, 4.

83 Petrie, *Athribis*, 4, pl. X. Kanawati, *El-Hagarsa* I, 60, pls. 43.

84 Petrie, *Athribis*, pl. XII.

85 Cf. the photographs published in Kanawati, *El-Hagarsa* I, pls. 12–13.

86 The following is based on El-Sayed, in El-Sayed and El-Masry (eds), *Athribis* I, 1–89.

87 The site is never referred to in Arabic sources as 'Tall Atrīb', which is exclusively used for the lower Egyptian Athribis.

88 For a comprehensive characterisation of the site see El-Sayed and El-Masry, *Athribis* I; El-Sayed, in *Fs Thissen*.

89 Not listed in Ramzī, *Qāmūs*. Aš-Šayḫ Ḥamad is classified as nağʿ/hamlet by Boinet Bey, *Dictionnaire Géographique*, 143, with 397 inhabitants in 1899.

90 See note 121. Nağʿ aš-Šayḫ Ḥamad is today affiliated to the county of Wannīna aš-šarqīya.

91 PM V, 31.

92 See El-Sayed and El-Masry, *Athribis* I, 71–73.

93 This paragraph presents in summary the comprehensive discussion in El-Sayed, in *Fs Thissen*, 523–526; cf. also El-Sayed, in El-Sayed and El-Masry (eds), *Athribis* I, 3–9.

94 A. H. Gardiner, 'The supposed Athribis of Upper Egypt', *JEA* 31 (1945), 108–111. For Lower Egyptian Athribis see H. Szymanska, *Terres cuites d'Athribis*, (MRE 12; Turnhout 2005).

probably 'Athribis' was founded before the Middle Kingdom, but experienced its heyday in late Ptolemaic and early Roman times when two extraordinary building projects were undertaken: a temple with a huge pylon built in the reign of Ptolemy IX and another, much larger temple dedicated to the Triad of Panopolis by Ptolemy XII.

The site is, moreover, of crucial importance for the Christian history of the area, since the western mountain, the temple precinct, and parts of the village were occupied in late antiquity by a monastic community, mostly comprised of nuns, affiliated with the nearby 'White Monastery federation'. The Temple of Ptolemy XII (see below), the main feature of the site, was converted at the end of the fourth century AD into a huge dye works belonging to the nunnery that by that time had expanded into and around the temple precinct.

The history of scientific exploration began in 1825 when John Gardner Wilkinson[95] was the first to copy a Greek dedicatory inscription on one of the broken lintels in the pronaos of the Temple of Ptolemy XII. Nestor L'Hôte paid a visit in 1839 and sketched the speos[96] located in the central part of the necropolis.[97] The facade of the same speos, which half a century later escaped the notice of the BSAE mission, was recorded again in 1845 when the Prussian Expedition, led by Lepsius, spent a day surveying the site.[98] The excavations, conducted by Petrie in the winter of 1907/08, were the first to result in the recording, though partial, of the two major Ptolemaic temples and some other features at the site as well. Excavations were resumed in 1981 by an EAO/SCA mission directed at first by Rifat El-Farrag and after his death in 1984 by Yahia El-Masry.[99] In 2003 a German Egyptian mission initiated by Yahia El-Masry and the author resumed field work with the aim of finally providing a comprehensive record of the site's topography, archaeological remains,[100] and an epigraphic record,[101]simultaneously developing and implementing a conservation plan for the endangered monuments.[102] During nearly a century after Petrie left the site, it had been altered considerably with few of the changes properly recorded.

2.3.2 Repography of recordings

Although an inconsistent record of the results achieved during the 1907/08 season at the monumental site of Athribis-Atrīpe, Petrie's general plan of the site and his plan view of the Temple of Ptolemy XII (Auletes) is reproduced and briefly commented upon here.

PMAN 591 is a reprography of Pl. XIV in the published report showing the monuments explored. The scale is 1:2000. The monuments Petrie explored on the mound included on the plan are: 1) Temple of Ptolemy XII (Auletes)[103], 2) Temple of Ptolemy IX (Physkon)[104], 3) Gate of Ptolemy IX (Physkon)[105], 4) 'Roman chapel'[106], 5) 'monastery'[107] and 6) 'dye house'[108]. Those situated in the necropolis of rock-cut tombs are: 7) 'zodiac[109] tomb', 8) 'north

95 El-Sayed, in El-Sayed and El-Masry (eds), *Athribis* I, 46–48.
96 El-Sayed, in El-Sayed and El-Masry (eds), *Athribis* I, 13–14.
97 Lepsius identified the structure as a tomb, see El-Sayed, in El-Sayed and El-Masry (eds), *Athribis* I, 48–50.
98 El-Sayed, in El-Sayed and El-Masry (eds), *Athribis* I, 53–55
99 Farag et al, *MDAIK* 41, 1–8.
100 R. El-Sayed and J. Kosciuk, 'Archaeological and Topographic Survey: Site nomenclature and numeration systems', in El-Sayed and El-Masry (eds), *Athribis* I, 92–94; J. Kosciuk, 'Architectural Survey and Recording', in El-Sayed and El-Masry (eds), *Athribis* I, 94–96; R. Staiger, H. J. Przybilla and E. Büttner, 'Geodetic Surveying Methods', in El-Sayed and El-Masry (eds), *Athribis* I, 98–105.
101 R. El-Sayed and Y. El-Masry, 'Epigraphic Survey and Recording', in El-Sayed and El-Masry (eds), *Athribis* I, 97.
102 H. Leisen, C. Verbeek and E. von Plehwe-Leisen, 'Konservierung von Stein und Wandmalerei im Tempel Ptolemaios' XII. in Athribis', in El-Sayed and El-Masry (eds), *Athribis* I, 220–277. The elaborate conservation plan was, however, until the present not implemented and priority was given to further excavating the Temple of Ptolemy XII for the sake of further epigraphic recording.
103 Petrie, *Athribis*, 4–7; El-Sayed and El-Masry, *Athribis* I, 18–30, 107–108; El-Sayed, in *Fs Thissen*, 519–538.
104 Petrie, *Athribis*, 10–11; El-Sayed and El-Masry, *Athribis* I, 18, 113–114, 117, 213.
105 Petrie, *Athribis*, 11; El-Sayed and El-Masry, *Athribis* I, 110–113, 149–197.
106 Petrie, *Athribis*, 11; El-Sayed and El-Masry, *Athribis* I, 58, 113.
107 Petrie, *Athribis*, 11; J. Kosciuk, 'The Architectural Record', in El-Sayed and El-Masry (eds), *Athribis* I, 108–109; El-Sayed, in *Fs Thissen*, 536–537.
108 Petrie, *Athribis*, 11; El-Sayed and El-Masry, *Athribis* I, 58.
109 Petrie, *Athribis*, 12–13; El-Sayed & El-Masry, *Athribis* I, 20–21, 59.

tomb' (Tomb of Psenosiris)[110] and 9) tomb[111] with a Greek inscription on the facade. The features investigated by Petrie but omitted from the plan are: a) quarries[112] and b) a stone block[113] nearby with a relief depicting gods. The most noteworthy feature unmentioned by Petrie is the speos among the rock-cut tombs recorded by Lepsius and L'Hôte (cf. above).[114]

Petrie's site plan moreover shows features that could not be traced during the more recent surveys. Either they are today no longer extant or were theoretical constructions, inferred by Petrie. Or perhaps they must be explained simply as 'ghost features', products of confusion. The most obvious among them is the eastern wing of the *temenos*[115] wall with the Gateway of Ptolemy IX. Petrie shows two thick sections of masonry abutting the doorjambs and another long, thin southern wing of the *temenos* wall. The plan is also missing one monumental feature still preserved today that must have been visible during the 1907/08 season: the huge sections of a mud brick *temenos*[116] wall southeast of the Temple of Ptolemy IX **(pl. VIIIc)**. Possibly this wall was simply displaced on the plan, erroneously connected to the stone gate by Petrie.[117] Unfortunately no general view could be identified among the PMAN showing this part of the site.

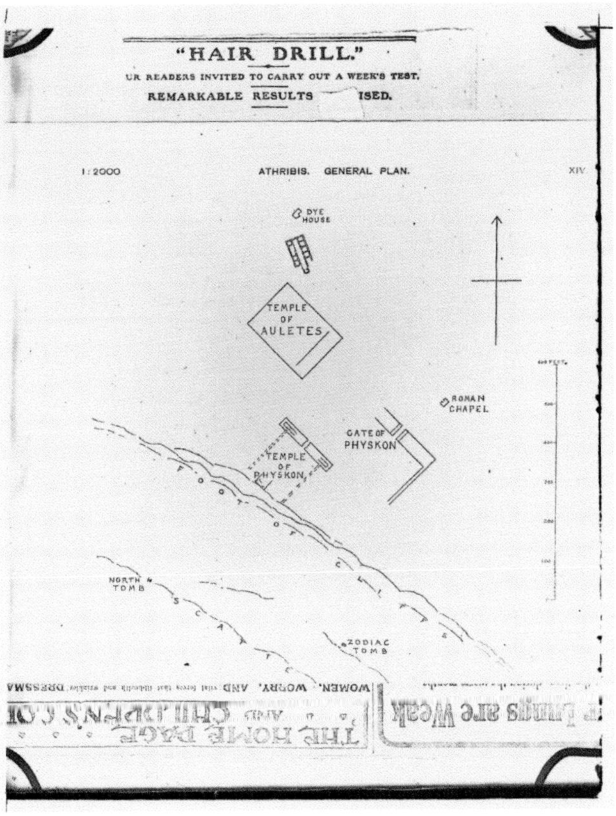

PMAN 591
Athribis-Atrīpe, Petrie's 'General Plan' of the site = Petrie, Athribis, pl. XIV, notation reading 'ATH. XIV'.

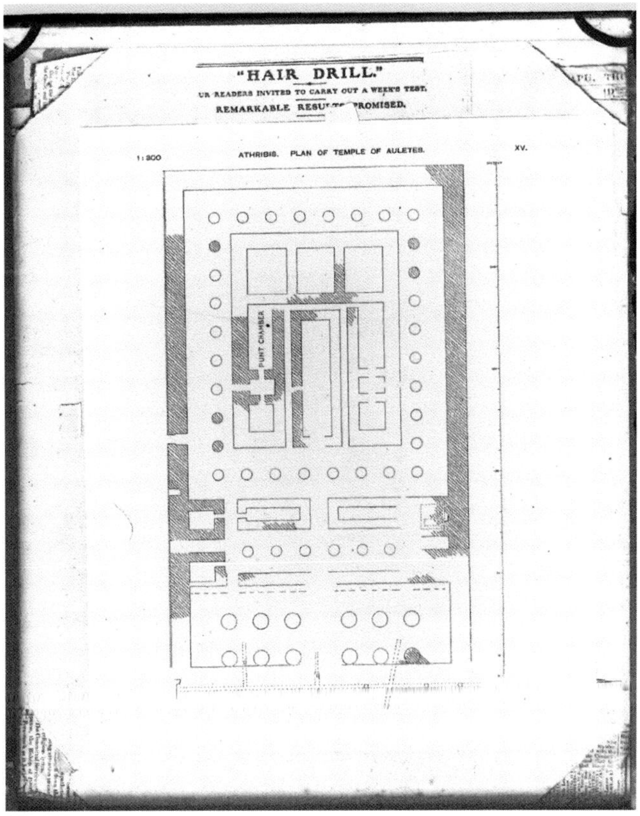

PMAN 592
Athribis-Atrīpe, Petrie's 'Plan of the Temple of [Ptolemy XII] *Auletes', notation reading 'ATH. XV'.*

110 Petrie, *Athribis*, 13; Farag et al., *MDAIK* 41, 1–8; El-Sayed and El-Masry, *Athribis* I, 20, 59.
111 Petrie, *Athribis*, 13; Farag et al., *MDAIK* 41, 1–8; El-Sayed and El-Masry, *Athribis* I, 46, 60 (fig. 128).
112 Petrie, *Athribis*, 13; El-Sayed and El-Masry, *Athribis* I, 71, 73.
113 See Petrie, *Athribis*, 5; El-Sayed and El-Masry, *Athribis* I, 35.
114 Lepsius, *LD* Text II, 161; Farag et al., *MDAIK* 41, 1–8; El-Sayed and El-Masry, *Athribis* I, 14, 20, 52–55.
115 Petrie, *Athribis*, 11; El-Sayed and El-Masry, *Athribis* I, 110–111.
116 See El-Sayed and El-Masry, *Athribis* I, 74, 111–112, 116–117, 141 (fig. 2.3.39).
117 For discussion see El-Sayed and El-Masry, *Athribis* I, 74.

PMAN 592: The plan shows the results of the architectural recording of the temple which was not completely excavated – only the walls designated by hatching were traced. Significantly, they are the tallest walls preserved. The remaining features are hypothetical reconstructions, as is clearly recognisable when they are compared to the more recent plan reproduced here on **pl. XIII**. The dotted lines south of the pronaos façade indicate the course of the drainage system belonging to the phase of reuse in late Roman times.[118]

2.3.3 Site views

The documentary value of the site views has been noted above. However, those views lacking clear reference points allow only tentative attribution and orientation. This is the case with PMAN 623, 633, 618, 631, 621.

PMAN 623
Athribis-Atrīpe. View of the promontory of Mount Atrīpe, no notation.

The view of the promontory of 'Mount Atrīpe' is from the low desert ground looking north (?). The exact position of the photographer is uncertain but was most probably half way between the sites of Athribis-Atrīpe and al-Haǧāri-sa. The photograph was presumably taken on the same walk as PMAN 633, since the same wooden walking staff is present on both; in PMAN 623 it can be seen leaning against a fallen rock in the lower left hand corner.

118 El-Sayed, in *Fs Thissen*, 535.

PMAN 633
Athribis-Atrīpe. View looking out of a rock-cut tomb in the necropolis, no notation.

The photograph was taken on a misty day at the mouth of a cave or one of the rock-cut tombs in the necropolis at Athribis-Atrīpe. The focal point is a strange eroded geological formation in the centre. The walking staff as in PMAN 623 leans against the exterior of the rock face.

PMAN 622: This is a distant view, looking east over the Nile Valley from the top of the mountain at al-Haǧārisa [**cf. pl. VIb**]. The photographer seems to be at the valley separating Mount Atrīpe from the mountain of al-Haǧārisa. At the farthest end the eastern mountain chain is clearly visible behind the riverbed at Aḫmīm where the Nile makes its distinctive double change of course. The plain on the western bank in the centre seems to be the focal point of the shot. The silhouette of the town of Sūhāǧ[119] [26°32'51''N/31°41'56''E] located next to the river bank is clearly recognisable. On the plain the villages of Wannīna al-ġarbīya[120] [26°31'03''N/31°40''53''E] and Wannīna aš-šarqīya[121] [26°31'31''N/31°41'01''E] (to the left) as well as al-Maḥāmida[122] [26°30'51''N/31°41'34''E] and Rawāfiʿ al-Quṣayr[123] [26°31'10''N/31°42'13''E] (to the right) can be distinguished.

119 Ramzī, *Qāmūs*, 128. Sūhāǧ, then capital of the Province of Ǧirǧā, according to Boinet Bey, *Dictionnaire Géographique*, 504 with 13.930 (including suburbs: 14.512) inhabitants in 1899.

120 Ramzī, *Qāmūs*, 134. Wannīna al-ġarbīya is classified as nāḥiya/village by Boinet Bey, *Dictionnaire Géographique*, 530 with 2.673 inhabitants in 1899.

121 Ramzī, *Qāmūs*, 134. Wannīna aš-šarqīya is classified as nāḥiya/village by Boinet Bey, *Dictionnaire Géographique*, 530 with 1.309 (including suburbs: 1.706) inhabitants in 1899.

122 Ramzī, *Qāmūs*, 131. al-Maḥāmida is classified as nāḥiya/village by Boinet Bey, *Dictionnaire Géographique*, 348 with 1.662 (including suburbs: 1.880) inhabitants in 1899.

123 Ramzī, *Qāmūs*, 133. Rawāfiʿ al-Quṣayr is classified as nāḥiya/village by Boinet Bey, *Dictionnaire Géographique*, 462 with 2.899 (including suburbs: 3.505) inhabitants in 1899.

PMAN 622
Mount Atrīpe. View from the top of the mountain overlooking the Nile Valley between the sites of al-Haǧārisa and Aḫmīm, looking east, no notation.

PMAN 631
Mount Atrīpe. View from the top of the mountain into the Libyan Desert, looking west, no notation.

It is not quite clear from which position this view was taken. However, it doubtless shows a view into the high plateau of the Libyan Desert looking west. For a modern view of the high desert at Athribis-Atrīpe see **pl. VIa**.

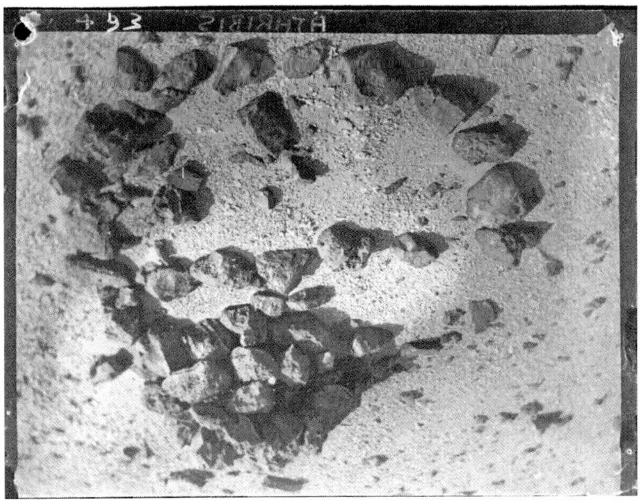

PMAN 617
'Mount Atrīpe' (?). Circularly arranged pile of stones on desert ground, notation reading 'ATHRIBIS' and '493' (mirrored).

PMAN 621
'Mount Atrīpe' (?). Rock and pebbles in the western mountain, no notation.

PMAN 617 shows stone chips on the desert ground, piled up in a circular-like arrangement. Similar features are extant on the high desert plateau of Mount Atrīpe, although it remains unclear if the photograph actually illustrates such features, making the attribution of PMAN 617 uncertain. The notations were written on both sides of the glass.

Likewise uncertain is the location of the view on PMAN 621. The photograph shows a cleft in the rock filled with pebbles that appear to have slid down from an upper stratum. The pebbles are appropriate for a location on or near the mountain plateau.

PMAN 632

Athribis-Atrīpe. General view of the northernmost end of the mound, looking northeast, no notation.

Identification of details in PMAN 632 is made well-nigh impossible due to overexposure but comparison with PMAN 627 leaves little doubt that the focus is the village of Naǧʿ aš-Šayḫ Ḥamad at the northeast end of the mound.

PMAN 627, a general view of the northern part of the mound, was taken from a position halfway up the western mountain at Athribis-Atrīpe. In the distance the silhouette of the eastern mountain chain near Aḫmīm is recognisable below a cloudy sky. To the left the village of Naǧʿ aš-Šayḫ Ḥamad – which at that time consisted only of a few houses, the related Muslim cemetery and palm groves – are visible. In 1908 the cultivated plain in the background was nearly void of habitation, as shown in the photograph; in the interim it has been in large part uncontrolledly developed.

The northern part of the mound where the excavations were concentrated is the focal point of the photograph. The partially exposed Temple of Ptolemy XII is delineated by debris and the brightness of its limestone walls. The pale walls of the exposed 'Punt chamber' to the rear of the ruins are distinguishable from the more brownish debris of the uppermost stratum. Several test excavations are visible north of the temple, along with the exposed dye works and the 'monastery'. The pylon of the Temple of Ptolemy IX was under excavation simultaneously. Clearly recognisable is a row of workmen carrying debris out of a deep pit, east of the pylon, which might be the trench shown in PMAN 628 and 629 (see below). In the eastern part of the mound the same two tents that occur in PMAN 624 and 630 are present. The Gateway of Ptolemy IX, the temenos wall and the 'Roman chapel' – all located in the southern sector of the site – were unfortunately not caught on this or any other photograph among the Petrie Museum archives. PMAN 627 is a unique record of the site during the 1907/08 season.

PMAN 627
Athribis-Atrīpe. View of the mound looking east, taken from half way up the mountain, no notation.

PMAN 629
Athribis-Atrīpe. General view of the northern part of the mound with rock-tombs in the background, looking west, no notation.

PMAN 629: This view of the site was taken from a position at the eastern fringe of the mound. In the centre the debris from the excavations of the dye works and the 'monastery' can be seen with rock-cut tombs and quarries visible in the background. On one print, made from the same negative, there is written in Petrie's hand: "Quarries of Athribis".

PMAN 624
Athribis-Atrīpe. View of the mound with camp, looking northeast, no notation.

PMAN 630
Athribis-Atrīpe. View of the mound with camp, looking northeast, no notation.

PMAN 624 and 630 show identical views of the mound. Both photographs were taken on the same cloudy day. The photographer stood close to the site of the 'Roman chapel' in the southern part of the site. The two tents appearing on most views of the site are here in the lower left corner. On the hillock in the centre of the photograph, test trenches and a hut made of reeds (housing for the workmen?) are discernable.

2.3.4 Monuments

The Temple of Ptolemy XII (Auletes)

The monument referred to as '*Temple of Auletes*' in Petrie's report constitutes the most significant feature of the site. Dedicated to Min, Repit, and Kolanthes, the 'Triad of Panopolis,'[124] the temple was commissioned by Ptolemy XII Neos Dionysos, nicknamed Auletes, who ruled Egypt from 80 to 58 BC and again from 55 to 51 BC.[125] The

124 El-Sayed, in El-Sayed and El-Masry (eds), *Athribis* I, 10–13; C. Leitz, 'Le temple de Ptolémée XII à Athribis – un temple pour Min(-Re) ou pour Repit?', *BSFE* 172 (2008), 32–52; D. Mendel, 'Die Soubassements der Säulen im Tempel von Athribis: Die Götter von Chemmis', in A. Rickert und B. Ventker (eds), *Altägyptische Enzyklopädien. Die Soubassements in den Tempeln der griechisch-römischen Zeit. Soubassementstudien* I,2, (SSR 7; Wiesbaden 2014), 828.

125 On his reign see G. Hölbl, *Geschichte des Ptolemäerreiches. Politik, Ideologie und religiöse Kultur von Alexander dem Großen bis zur römischen Eroberung*, (Darmstadt, 1994), 195–205 and W. Huss, *Ägypten in hellenistischer Zeit, 332–30 v. Chr.*, (München, 2001), 671–702. The building project was probably started during the first reign of Ptolemy XII - see V. Altmann, 'Zu den in Athribis nachgewiesenen ptolemäischen Königen und römischen Kaisern' in El-Sayed and El-Masry (eds), *Athribis* I, 208. PM, V, 31, based on R. Weill, 'Koptos. Relation sommaire des travaux executés par MM. Ad. Reinach', *ASAE* 11 (1911), 105 (n. 2) and idem, 'La titulature

PMAN 593

Athribis-Atrīpe. Temple of Ptolemy XII, lintel above passage from F5 to L3, notation reading: 'ATH XIX'; 'N° I'.

Fig. 1: *Athribis-Atrīpe. Temple of Ptolemy XII, lintel above passage from F5 to L3, line drawing.*

plan of the temple covers an area 45 by 75 metres, making it equal in size to the Temple of Dendara. The plan could be verified by the EAO/SCA mission that between 1981 and 1996 excavated about three-quarters of the temple remains which had been buried under debris at the end of Petrie's campaign.[126] From 2003 to 2008, the remains, as far as accesible, were recorded in detail by the German Egyptian mission under the author's direction.[127] The floor plan resulting from the work of both missions, differs essentially from Petrie's, based as it was on partial, clearance and certain unfounded assumptions.[128] In his report Petrie gave the following explanation for not excavating the temple completely:[129]

> *A complete clearance was not attempted for several reasons. It would be premature to bare the sculptures that remain until it is settled whether they shall be protected in place or removed. And we had no time or money to spare for the great clearance which would be needed. But enough was exposed to make a plan of the main features, and to copy most of the inscriptions and scenes that are worth notice. It was then covered over again to protect it, after removing (by Professor Maspero's permission) one*[130] *figure of Auletes, which belonged to a scene almost destroyed, and a few of the innumerable figures of nomes which were carved round all the walls inside and outside.*

PMAN 593: A detail of this extraordinarily sharp photograph of the lintel above the doorway giving access from room F5[131] to the western ambulatory L3 was reproduced on Pl. XIX in Petrie's report. The reliefs are nowadays nearly completely destroyed.[132] PMAN 593 is another valuable record of the fragile sculptures that fell victim to superstition and quarrying in antiquity; in modern times, they continue to be threatened by looting and exposure to weathering. A line drawing based on the photograph is reproduced as **figure 1**.

PMAN 618: In the centre, the southeast part of the so-called 'Punt-chamber', the 'laboratory' of the temple of Ptolemy XII can be seen. Some of the incense trees depicted in the *soubassements* on the east wall are visible (see PMAN 594 and 601 further below). The greater part is obscured by debris left in the centre of the room. The remains of the sanctuary at the top left corner of the photograph are still covered entirely with debris and only the northernmost part of the *couloir mysterieux* C5 is partially exposed. The nome figures preserved in the reliefs on the *soubassement* of the east wall of C5 are visible (see PMAN 595 below). The photograph is good evidence for Petrie's practice of digging alongside the walls and leaving most of the interior of the structure hidden by debris. At the right margin of the photograph some ceramic vessels placed up against the wall are discernible

PMAN 594 and 601 show the reliefs of the *soubassement* on the eastern wall in chamber F6[133] which depict incense trees in different stages of growth during the seasonal cycle. Only PMAN 594 was chosen for the publication. The views could not be taken directly in front of the wall since the chamber had not been cleared, preventing placement of the camera in an appropriate position (cf. PMAN 618, above).

---

pharaonique de Ptolémé César et ses monuments de Koptos', *Rec Trav* 34 (1912), 86 erroneously ascribes the Temple to Ptolemy XVI (sic) Caesar. Cf. Altmann, in El-Sayed and El-Masry (eds), *Athribis* I, 201 (n. 201).

126 El-Masry, *MDAIK* 57 (2001), 212 (fig. 4).

127 Kosciuk, in El-Sayed and El-Masry (eds), *Athribis* I, 94–96, pl. IX. See **pl. XIII** in this publication.

128 Such as, for example, the idea of Greek influence on the architecture that must be rejected, see Petrie, *Athribis*, 7.

129 Petrie, *Athribis*, 5.

130 Effectively, Petrie removed not less than 20 blocks of at least three sceenes. Cf. the forthcoming third segment of the study.

131 Cf. the numbering system used on **pl. XIII**.

132 C. Leitz, D. Mendel and Y. El-Masry, *Die Außenwände und westlichen Seitenkapellen des Tempels von Athribis*, vol I, (Le Caire: IFAO, 2013), 229–230, 235–236, vol. 2, Taf. 128 published as C. Leitz, D. Mendel and M. el-Bialy, *Die Außenwände und westlichen Seitenkapellen des Tempels von Athribis*, (Cairo: MSA, 2015), vol. I, 229–230, 235–236, vol. 2, Taf. 128.

133 C. Leitz, D. Mendel and Y. El-Masry, *Außenwände*, (Le Caire: IFAO, 2013), vol. I, 245–250, vol. II, Taf. 134–136 = C. Leitz, D. Mendel and M. el-Bialy, *Außenwände*, (Cairo: MSA, 2015), vol. I, 245–250, vol. II, Taf. 134–136.

PMAN 618
Athribis-Atrīpe. Temple of Ptolemy XII. View showing the partially excavated 'Punt chamber' (F6) and corridor C5, looking southeast, no notation.

PMAN 594

Athribis-Atrīpe. Temple of Ptolemy XII, 'Punt chamber'(F6), incense trees, east wall, soubassement and lower band of inscription, notation reading 'ATH XIX'.

PMAN 601

Athribis-Atrīpe. Temple of Ptolemy XII, 'Punt chamber' (F6), incense trees, east wall, soubassement and lower band of inscription, no notation.

PMAN 595
Athribis-Atrīpe. Temple of Ptolemy XII, 'couloir mystérieux' C5, nome figures, notation reading 'ATH XIX'.

PMAN 602
Athribis-Atrīpe. Temple of Ptolemy XII, outer enclosure wall M1, central part, no notation.

PMAN 595: This photograph shows the *soubassement* in the western passage C5 of the *couloir mystérieux*, the ambulatory surrounding the sanctuary (**pl. XIII**). The scenes[134] depict a procession of nome figures in geographic order. The procession is led by the king who is depicted opposite a shrine (?) decorated with (?) an Wedjat-eye, which is barely discernable on PMAN 618. The blocks Petrie removed are today in the UK and continental European museums.[135]

PMAN 602: The photograph was taken from an elevated position east of the partly excavated temple enclosure wall (M1). The large refectory associated with the nunnery that had been installed in the temple precinct in late antiquity was discovered in the 1980s under the debris on which the camera stands in the photo.[136] The scene to the right shows the king (facing right) followed by his ka.[137] The continuation of this scene of the first register is seen on PMAN 603.

134 Cf. Leitz, Mendel, El-Masry, *Athribis* II.1, xxiii–xxv; 301–310 and *Athribis* II.3, 88–89.

135 Considered in the forthcoming third part of this study.

136 For a preliminary plan see El-Masry, *MDAIK* 57 (2001), 212 (fig. 4). For a full account on this refectory see R. El-Sayed and Y. El-Masry (eds), *Athribis Report 2008–2011* (forthcoming).

137 Petrie, *Athribis*, pls. XXIII–XXIV, XXX. Scene 53–55 in Leitz, Mendel and El-Masry, *Außenwände*, vol I, 65–72; published as Leitz, Mendel and el-Bialy, *Außenwände*, vol. I, 65–72.

PMAN 603

Athribis-Atrīpe. Temple of Ptolemy XII, outer enclosure wall M1, central part, no notation.

PMAN 603 was taken from the same position as PMAN 602. It shows the reliefs of the first register on the eastern enclosure wall M1.[138]

PMAN 604: This photograph was taken from an elevated position west of the Temple of Ptolemy XII. The camera stood on the surface where the remains of early Islamic period houses were recorded in 2010.[139] In the focal point of the shot is the lintel above the doorway reproduced in line drawing in the published report.[140] The photograph and drawing document the scene on the lintel completely preserved. By 1981 it had sustained severe damage, obviously caused by clandestine attempts to remove the reliefs (**pl. Va**).

PMAN 612: For this photo, the camera was placed on the debris in the northwest corner of the ruined temple. The view, southwards along the main axis of the temple, shows partially bared huge roofing slabs, fragmented capitals and lintels, scattered over the area of the eastern ambulatory L1. In the centre a tunnel is visible that Petrie's workmen dug below the blocks alongside the wall to facilitate the copying of inscriptions.[141] In the distance the promontory of Mount Atrīpe can be seen while in the upper left hand corner the eastern wing of the mud brick temenos[142] wall projects from the debris.

138 Petrie, *Athribis*, pls. XXIX, XXX. Scene 52–53 in Leitz, Mendel and El-Masry, *Aussenwände*, vol. I, 68–73, vol. II, Taf. 48–49; published as Leitz, Mendel and el-Bialy, *Außenwände*, vol. I, 68–73, vol. II, Taf. 48–49.

139 El-Sayed and El-Masry, *Athribis Report 2008–2011* (forthcoming).

140 Petrie, *Athribis*, pl. XXIX.

141 Petrie, *Athribis*, 5.

142 For this wall see now Kosciuk, in El-Sayed & El-Masry (eds), *Athribis* I, 107, 121 (fig. 2.3.2).

PMAN 604
Athribis-Atrīpe. Temple of Ptolemy XII, western outer enclosure wall M3, doorway to ambulatory L3, lintel, no notation.

PMAN 612

Athribis-Atrīpe. Temple of Ptolemy XII, ambualtory L1 and enclosure wall M1, view of the excavations looking south, no notation.

PMAN 620
Athribis-Atrīpe. Temple of Ptolemy XII, eastern enclosure wall M1 during excavation, workmen posing, no notation.

This photograph is one of the few to include Petrie's workmen. A group of four men with their tools beside them pose for the picture which was taken from the northeast to show the excavation of the northern part of the eastern ambulatory (L1). In the foreground the outer face of the eastern enclosure wall (M1) has been exposed for the most part. The stratification of the debris on top of the remains of the building clearly reflects the history of reuse and destruction of the temple:[143] below wind-blown sand, a thick layer consisting of limestone rubble, powdered lime, and a few crushed bricks is recognisable. The fill below consists mainly of organic waste and rubble. The quality of the photograph is excellent; only the faces of the workmen, who probably did not stand entirely still, are slightly blurred. In the upper centre of the photograph several tomb entrances are discernable, one of them the entrance to the 'zodiac tomb'.

PMAN 608 shows a view from the southwest of the pronaos of the Temple of Ptolemy XII. Huge roofing blocks and fragments of hathoric capitals project from the debris [cf. **pl. VIIa**]. (These monochrome photographs, of course, do not allow any comment on the polychromy of the painted capitals.)

PMAN 610 is a closeup view of two fragments of the hathoric capital visible in the centre of PMAN 608.

143 A summary of the history of reuse can be found in El-Sayed, in El-Sayed & El-Masry (eds), *Athribis* I, 212–217 and more comprehensively El-Sayed, in *Fs Thissen*, 519–538.

PMAN 608

Athribis-Atrīpe. Temple of Ptolemy XII, Pronaos, fragmented huge roofing blocks and capitals projecting from the debris, no notation.

PMAN 610

Athribis-Atrīpe. Temple of Ptolemy XII, pronaos, fragmented hathoric capitals scattered in the debris, no notation.

PMAN 611

Athribis-Atrīpe (?). Temple of Ptolemy XII (?), fragments of columns and building blocks, no notation.

PMAN 611 illustrating fragmented building blocks and columns in the midst of crushed limestone and debris is slightly overexposed. The association of the negative with Athribis-Atrīpe is, however, not certain.

PMAN 619

Athribis-Atrīpe. West of Temple of Ptolemy XII, workforce carrying debris to a dump, no notation.

This is another of the three photographs showing Petrie's Egyptian laborers at work. In the centre, carriers are busy tipping debris onto a huge dump. In the background the promontory of Mount Atrīpe extends into the view.

The Temple of Ptolemy IX (Physkon)

The monument referred to as the 'Temple of Physkon' in Petrie's report is one of the most striking features of the site. Very little of the temple proper could be discerned either by Petrie or during the 2003–2011 surface survey. The site is entirely covered with huge amounts of sherds and rubble.[144] The dimensions of the immense pylon that fronted the temple to the east could, however, be traced and plotted on the site map **(pl. XIV)**.[145] For a hypothetical plan based both on Petrie's plan and the results of the recent survey, see **pl. IX**. Petrie's attribution of this temple to Ptolemy IX Soter II 'Physkon'[146] could not, however, be confirmed during the recent survey. His account contains interesting details about architectural features which he partially uncovered; some are recognisable on the unpublished photographs presented below:[147]

> *The earlier temple at Athribis was that built by Ptolemy IX, nicknamed Physkon, two or three generations before the temple of* [scil. Ptolemy XII] *Auletes. On Pl. XIV will be seen the position of the great pylons of Physkon, which show all that remains of his building. Of the temple itself only some rock cutting and blocks of pavement were found at the back against the cliff.* [...]

> *The pylon of the temple was the part first uncovered.* [...] *Seeing a long line of chips in the ground I expected that it marked the rubbish thrown out in destroying a great stone wall. On clearing to the west of the chips for some days we found nothing but house ruins. At last it appeared as if rock existed at a high level there amid the ruins, and we worked round it for some days further, searching for foundations. But to our astonishment I found a joint beneath it, and our rock proved to be the immense roofing blocks of chambers within a pylon.* [...]

PMAN 613

Athribis-Atrīpe. Temple of Ptolemy IX, pylon, northern tower, view into the inner chamber 'B', taken from the south-west, no notation.

144 Kosciuk, in El-Sayed & El-Masry (eds), *Athribis* I, 113–114.

145 El-Sayed & El-Masry, *Athribis* I, pls. IV, V, VI, VII, VIIIa, c.

146 For Ptolemy IX see Hölbl, *Geschichte des Ptolemäerreiches*, 183–193; Huss, *Ägypten*, 627–641; S. Caßor-Pfeiffer, 'Zur Reflexion ptolemäischer Geschichte in den ägyptischen Tempeln aus der Zeit Ptolemaios IX. Philometor II./Soter II und Ptolemaios X. Alexander I. (116–80 v. Chr.). Teil 1: die Bau- und Dekorationstätigkeit', *JEH* 1,1 (2008), 21–77.

147 Petrie, *Athribis*, 10–11.

We then cleared deeply along the line of the pylon, and found the lower part of the gateway itself, with cartouches of Physkon. This gateway had been roughly blocked on the inner side, leaving only a narrow door of access. This points to the enclosure of the temple being completed, and intact after its disuse [...].

The south-eastern end of the pylon had been entirely destroyed; but it was evidently symmetrical, and is here, therefore, duplicated from the other end. [...] *There were no traces of inscriptions upon the chamber walls. The inner chamber was lighted by two long horizontal slits in the wall at the level of the top; widening embrasures led down from these, sloping steeply to near the chamber floor. Thus the inner end of the chamber was completely lighted.*

PMAN 613: This photograph, taken from a position immediately southwest of the pylon tower (**pl. IX**), provides a unique view into the interior of the northern tower. In the lower right hand corner, one roofing block is visible, fallen from its position presumably during the dismantling process in late antiquity. In the upper left hand corner the southernmost roofing block of those still *in situ* can be seen. In the eastern wall of the tower the horizontal slit mentioned by Petrie is visible. North of the slit there are two square openings lower down in the wall, which Petrie did not comment upon; presumably they are niches for lamps.[148] The doorway connecting the central inner chamber with the northern inner chamber of the tower is also clearly visible, below its slightly projecting lintel. From the picture it can be presumed that stone of the same quality was employed for the walls as for the roofing blocks. The surface of the inner chamber seems, in fact, to have been undecorated.

PMAN 628

Athribis-Atrīpe (?). Temple of Ptolemy IX, southern tower of pylon (?), no notation.

148 Cf. U. Fauerbach, *Der große Pylon des Horus-Tempels von Edfu. Eine bauforscherische Untersuchung* (PhD thesis, University of Bamberg; Bamberg 2005), 134.

PMAN 609
Athribis-Atrīpe (?). Temple of Ptolemy IX, southern tower of pylon (?), no notation.

The attribution of PMAN 628 and 609 to a particular monument at the site of Athribis-Atrīpe is not quite certain, even though the Temple of Ptolemy IX seems to be a probable candidate for the subject. Both photographs show the same deep trench dug into the debris exposing the remains of an elongated stone structure built of ashlars. PMAN 628 was taken from halfway up the access ramp of the trench looking down to the stone structure. The view reveals the three towering faces of the trench to be composed of dense accumulations of dark debris, composed of organic material, pottery sherds, and a huge amount of flint pebbles, but noticeably few limestone chips. This stratification suggests a location outside the ruins of the Temple of Ptolemy XII where the stratification shows a quite different composition.[149]

PMAN 609 is a closeup view of the stone structure that looks very much like the foundation of a building, probably the southern tower of the pylon that was only partially excavated by Petrie. This assumption is supported by Petrie's remark, cited above, that the southern tower was destroyed. As documented by **pl. VIIb** the southernmost edge of the southern tower is preserved to some extent. It was only partially cleared during the EAO/SCA excavations in the 1990s; the central part remains buried below towering accumulations of debris. PMAN 609 probably shows this middle section of the tower dismanteled down to the lowermost row of ashlars, thus providing insight into the foundations that probably served as crypts. This assumption is supported by the opening forced in the floor visible on the left hand side of the photograph.

The Gate of Ptolemy IX 'Physkon'

The monument referred to as '*Gate of Physkon*'[150] and '*Outer Pylon/Gateway of Physkon*'[151] in Petrie's publication has been recently investigated in-depth and explained as the main entrance to the precinct of Repit [**cf. pl. VIIIa, b**].[152] Petrie himself had already recognized that this was the function of the structure:

149 Cf. PMAN 620.
150 Petrie, *Athribis*, pl. XIV.
151 Petrie, *Athribis*, pl. XXXV.
152 El-Sayed and El-Masry, *Athribis* I, 10, 74, 110–114.

> [...] *I had seen the gateway in the temenos to the east, and was searching for the temple which that had enclosed.* [...][153]
> *22. The temenos of this temple* [scil. the Temple of Ptolemy IX] *was entered by a gate to one side of the temple axis.* [...]. *The temenos gateway remains complete up to about five feet high. The inscriptions on these four faces are given in Pls. XXXI to XXXIV. Each face was probably similar to that on Pl. XXXII, with a band of inscription above it, and scenes above that. Hence, scarcely anything has been lost from the tops of the columns, and the defects are all in the effacement of the text by decay.* [...][154]

The plan Petrie included on Pl. XXXV, together with the unpublished photographs PMAN 596 and 607, prove that only the external western and eastern faces of the gate were cleared during the 1907/08 excavation. Neither the inscriptions[155] on the reveals nor an archaeological record of the interior was recorded. Petrie did not realise that, as in the case of the pylon of the Temple of Ptolemy IX (see above), the passageway through the gate had been walled up and blocked in later times. This must be interpreted as showing that the *temenos* wall was standing when the gate in the pylon was blocked.[156] In 2003 when the German-Egyptian mission began recording the gate, the remains of the blocking had been removed, apparently at some point during the work of the Egyptian mission at the site from 1981 to 1996 since it was recorded on the plan[157] and in photography **(pl. Vb)** made at that time.

PMAN 596
Athribis-Atrīpe. Gate of Ptolemy IX, east face, southern door frame, no notation.

153 Petrie, *Athribis*, 10.
154 Petrie, *Athribis*, 11.
155 On these see C. Leitz, R. El-Sayed, D. Mendel and Y. El-Masry, 'Die Inschriften des Torbaus Ptolemaios' IX.' in El-Sayed and El-Masry (eds.), *Athribis* I, 149–197.
156 Petrie, *Athribis*, 11. The situation got mixed up in Y. El-Masry, 'More Recent Excavations at Athribis in Upper Egypt', *MDAIK* 57 (2001), 209.
157 El-Masry, *MDAIK* 57, 209 (fig. 3).

PMAN 607

Athribis-Atrīpe. Gate of Ptolemy IX, east face, northern door frame, no notation.

PMAN 596: This unpublished photograph shows the feature as it existed in 1907/08. The decorated face of the uppermost ashlar with the lower part of a striking male deity visible on the photograph, was entirely decayed in 1981 when the EAO mission resumed work at the site.[158] Most of the structure is buried under debris and sand on the photograph. Neither on this photograph nor on PMAN 607 are any remains recognizable of the mud brick walls that originally must have abutted the stone masonry of the gate. This temenos wall seems to have been already substantially destroyed. Just as in the line drawings published by Petrie, the unpublished photograph is evidence that the inscriptions in 1907/08 were in much better condition than in 2003 when they were re-recorded by the German- Egyptian mission.[159]

PMAN 607: To keep the inscribed face clear of loose debris during recording, retaining walls of rubble and brick were erected by Petrie's workmen. The reliefs have suffered severe damage since the photograph was taken. Today, the inscriptions[160] are hardly legible. The unpublished photographs PMAN 596 and 607 represent important records of the monument's deterioration which will be no longer preventable.[161]

158 See **pl. VIIIa, b**.

159 On the inscriptions of the southern door frames of the eastern facade see Leitz, El-Sayed, Mendel and El-Masry, in El-Sayed and El-Masry (eds), *Athribis* I, 152–157.

160 For them see Leitz, El-Sayed, Mendel and El-Masry, in El-Sayed and El-Masry (eds), *Athribis* I, 158–161.

161 Much to the authors regret the elaborate conservation plan worked out during the period 2003–2008 by a distinguished team of conservation scientists from Cologne University for Applied Sciences was not implemented.

'Roman chapel'

Petrie briefly commented on the remains of another 'minor' monument that has completely disintegrated in the interim. In his report, he called it '*chapel of Roman age*' or simply '*Roman chapel*':[162]

> *23. Below that is the plan of a chapel of Roman age, the position of which is shown on Pl. XIV, at the side of the approach to the gate of Physkon. It is covered with long scenes of gods, and the work is so rough that it was not worth copying. The interior was not cleared out.*

Pertrie's attribution of the structure to the Roman Period was obviously based on the wall decoration. The plan of the building given on his Pl. XXXV shows a one-room building with an opening in the north wall and a *Rundstab* at all four corners. For a reconstruction of the plan based on Petrie's sketch and the recently conducted architectural recording, see **Pl. XI**.

Today, all that remains of the structure *in situ* is its stone foundation **(pl. VIIc)**. Traces of a relief showing a figure (presumably a deity) on a single isolated block do not suit the scenes shown in PMAN 606. The location of the chapel next to the *dromos* that once connected the main entrance of the temple precinct with a presumed quay at the eastern fringe of the town suggests that the building was a way-station where the sacred bark might repose in the course of processions.[163]

PMAN 606
Athribis-Atrīpe. 'Roman Chapel' (?), decorated western (?) face, no notation.

The unpublished photograph shows a view of the exterior wall of a stone structure built of ashlars and decorated with scenes and inscriptions in sunk relief. The building which is here preserved up to five rows of ashlars is partial-

162 Petrie, *Athribis*, 11.
163 On the quay see, Kosciuk, in El-Sayed and El-Masry (eds), *Athribis* I, 112; on the relationship of the temple precincts at Athribis and Aḫmīm cf. El-Sayed, in El-Sayed and El-Masry (eds), *Athribis* I, 10.

ly buried under debris. Clearly visible is the *Rundstab* at the right side of the picture. This distinctive architectural element and the evidence of the ritual scenes undoubtedly identify the building as a sanctuary of some kind. The style in which the scenes are executed is unrelated to any known reliefs in the Temple of Ptolemy XII, as is also true of the *Rundstab*. The remaining decoration consists of two superposed registers separated by the *bandeau du soubassement*. Both registers depict processions, the lower with animal-headed anthropomorphic deities (primeval gods ?) and the upper with priests, gods, and the king involved in a cultic (festival?) procession. The only decorated building that this photograph may relate to is the 'Roman chapel'(see above). Petrie's few comments on that chapel are, however, insufficient for a definite connection of it with PMAN 606.

The dye works

There are two buildings constructed of combined mud brick and burnt brick masonry among the structures Petrie excavated northeast of the Temple of Ptolemy XII dating to the site's occupation during late antiquity. Petrie described one of them as an '*early type of monastery*'.[164] He excavated it only partially, clearing mainly the interior. The plan published on Pl. XXXV of his report is accordingly preliminary. The building was again only partially surveyed in 2005 and tentatively explained by the author of this article as an infirmary **(pl. XII)**.[165] It was not photographed in detail in 1907/08, but is visible from afar on the general view of the site on PMAN 627 (see above).

The second building was identified by Petrie as a dyer's workshop (**pl. X**); only a plan of it was included in the publication. Fortunately several views of this building are extant among the unpublished PMA negatives. Petrie's description of the building, of which no reliably identifiable remains could be traced during the 2003–2011 survey,[166] reads:[167]

> *24. At the base of Pl. XXXV is the plan of a dyer's workshop, shown on the general plan, Pl. XIV, at the top. The two entrances are to the south. One leads to a room with a large well in the middle, and a bench along the west wall. This wall was lined with tiles above the bench, probably to receive the splashing of water. North of the well was a square pit, about three feet deep. The sides were of very rough brickwork, uncemented; and it seems likely that it was lined with lead as a cistern. There are three vats in the bench on the north, and beyond the cistern the bench passes into the vat room, with sixteen vats in the raised bench around the sides. These vats are lined with cement, and deeply stained. Most of them are black-blue with indigo, and some are red. Samples of colour from each vat have been brought away for examination. In this northern room the roof was carried on two pillars. To the west was a room, probably for business with customers, and giving access by a stairway to the upper storey, now destroyed. The great quantity of weaver's waste found in the rubbish piled against the temple, shows that much manufacturing was done in the town; hence large dye-shops woul be required.*

Remarkably enough, down to the present no comparable structure has been excavated elsewhere in Egypt.[168] Apart from the dye works, the existence of extensive dyeing installations inside the Temple of Ptolemy XII indicates that the site was an important centre of textile industry in late antiquity.[169]

PMAN 626: In the background of this general overview the mountains north of the 'valley of Trifeion',[170] opposite the Shenute Monastery, are clearly distinguishable. When the photograph was taken, the eastern part of the dye works in the foreground was most probably already refilled with sand after the building's remains had been plotted.[171]

164 Petrie, *Athribis*, 11, pl. XXXV.

165 El-Sayed, in *Fs Thissen*, 536–537; Kosciuk, in: El-Sayed and El-Masry (eds), *Athribis* I, 109. Consideration of this building and the question of infirmaries is included in the forthcoming third part of this study.

166 In all likelihood, the tentative placement of Petrie's plan of the building in the 2008 general site plan (El-Sayed and El-Masry, *Athribis* I, pls. IV–VII, VIIIc) needs to be adjusted.

167 Petrie, *Athribis*, 11.

168 But for a possible dye factory at Dendara, see S. Cauville, 'Dendara: du sanatorium au trinctorium', *BSFE* 61 (2004), 28–40. For dyeing textiles and their use in Egypt, cf. R. Germer, *Die Textilfärberei und die Verwendung gefärbter Textilien im Alten Ägypten*, (ÄA 53; Wiesbaden, 1992). Where the samples taken by Petrie ended up, remains unknown to the author.

169 Kosciuk, in El-Sayed and El-Masry (eds), *Athribis* I, 108, 110.

170 On this toponymic expression see El-Sayed, in *Fs Thissen*, 525; El-Sayed, in El-Sayed and El-Masry (eds), *Athribis* I, 26.

171 This was probably due to a misunderstanding in the field. Cf. Petrie, *Athribis*, 8 for a similar misunderstnading concerning the photographic recording.

PMAN 626
Athribis-Atrīpe. Dye works, general view taken from southeast, no notation.

PMAN 614
Athribis-Atrīpe. Dye works, view of the 'vat room', looking north, no notation.

PMAN 615

Athribis-Atrīpe. Dye works, general view of the room with well and cistern, looking southwest, no notation.

PMAN 616

Athribis-Atrīpe. Dye works, general view of the workshop's centre, looking east, no notation.

PMAN 614: The photograph of what Petrie termed the '*vat room*' is slightly out of focus. The base of one of the two pillars that presumably supported the roof is clearly discernible in the middle of the photograph, above, 16 vats built against the outer walls of the room are also shown.

PMAN 615: The high definition photograph shows a large well and cistern with four attached vats occupying the southeastern room of the dye works.[172] The entrance to the room is visible in the upper lefthand corner. The thickness of the wall separating the room with the well from the room to the east supports the idea of a second storey, suggested as well by the presence of a staircase in the latter.

PMAN 616: The view was probably meant to capture the eastern part of the building with the small room and its staircase and most of the 'vat room'. Neither room is completely shown, however. The cistern of the room with the well in the middle can be seen in the center of the image. The focal point seems to be the eastern outer wall in the background. At the upper left, the remains of the mudbrick masonry of the staircase can be distinguished, and the stone base of a pillar originally supporting the roof can once more be clearly seen at the extreme right.

2.3.5 Finds

There are very few photographs of finds from the 1907/08 season among the PMA negatives. For the sake of completeness they are reproduced here with more comprehensive discussion reserved for the third instalment of this study.

PMAN 599
Athribis-Atrīpe. Limestone head of Ptolemy IX (?), notation reading 'MI 4.6 XLV'.

PMAN 600
Athribis-Atrīpe. Limestone head of Ptolemy IX (?) notation reading 'MI D.'

172 But only three are included in Petrie's plan!

PMAN 605
Athribis-Atrīpe (?). Memphis (?). Abydos (?). Limestone stela with offerings on altar, persea (?) tree and ear, no notation; attribution questionable.

PMAN 599 was chosen for reproduction on Pl. XLV in the published report, while PMAN 600 is an unpublished three-quarter view of the limestone sculpture which after the division went to the Manchester Museum in 1908, there accessioned as number 4816; see the appendix further below.

PMAN 605: It is not certain whether this photograph was taken at one of the Sūhāğ sites, but if so, then most probably at Athribis-Atrīpe. It cannot be ruled out, however, that the object was purchased by Petrie on the local antiquities market. The fragmentary limestone stela was propped up against a wooden box for photography. Only part of the left half of the round-topped stela is preserved. The scene in raised relief depicts a table laden with offerings topped with a floral bouquet (*Stabstrauss*) alongside a tree. The ear beneath the leafy branches of the tree assures assignement of the stela to the genre of so-called ear stelae.[173] Only some leafy branches remain of the tree which resembles a *persea* or sycamore.[174] Although this stela is not pictured on any plate in Petrie's Memphis volumes, it cannot ruled out that it originated there where he found many comparable ear stelae in 1908.[175]

III Conclusion

This initial study of a planned series aiming at reevaluating Petrie's 1907/08 dig season at three sites located at the escarpment of Mount Atrīpe in the Sūhāğ district has produced previously inaccessible material for analysis but also raised new questions. Because the notebooks are a particualry complex source, detailed consideration of them was omitted here. A closer look at the notebooks may yet yield additional insights but would demand further extensive research that seemed unreasonable in view of the anticipated results. The photographic record, on the other

173 For such stelae see most recently E.-E. Morgan, 'Ägyptische Ohrenstelen: Fragen und Antworten', *SAK* 39 (2010), 271–280.
174 Especially since no fruit is depicted, which prohibits a definite identification. I thank Konstantin C. Lakomy for his help with this issue.
175 Petrie, *Memphis* I, 7, pls. IX–XIII.

hand, sheds light on some aspects of Petrie's work that were only briefly reported in his publication. Apart from general views of the sites and the contemporaneous landscape in 1907/1908, the unpublished photographs include informative details about several monuments at Athribis-Atrīpe in particular, namely: the Temple of Ptolemy XII, the gateway of Ptolemy IX, the pylon of the Temple of Ptolemy IX, the 'Roman chapel', and the dye works. Sketches and only a few comments were included in the published report on all but the first monument so that the PMA negatives provide unique, significant documentation of monuments and archaeological contexts now irrevocably lost, partially deteriorated or threatened in the foreseeable future, along with artefacts that have suffered degradation as well in some cases. Regrettably, however, certain views whose preservation was anticipated might aid in clarifying inconsistencies in Petrie's report, are not to be found in the archives. Time will show whether additional searches in the archives or perhaps mere coincidence may turn up more negatives or other archival documents.

Credits

All PMA negatives and Pl. 2: courtesy of the Petrie Museum of Egyptian Archaeology, University College London. – Fig. 1: © Konstantin C. Lakomy. – Pl. 1: © Project Mîn-Panos [source of satellite images: ArcGIS online "Esri, DigitalGlobe, GeoEye, Earthstar Geographics, CNES/Airbus DS, USDA, USGS, AEX, Getmapping, Aerogrid, IGN, IGP, swisstopo, and the GIS User Community]. –Plate 3: © The Sohag Survey Project, Sydney. – Pl. 4 a: after U. Monneret de Villard, Les couvents près de Sohâg (Deyr el-Abiaḍ et Deyr el-Aḥmar), (Milan, 1925) vol. I, fig. 5. – Pl. 4 b and Pls. 5–8: © Yahia El-Masry. – Pls. 9–12: © Project Mîn-Panos. – Pl. 13: after El-Sayed & El-Masry, *Athribis* I, fig. 2.2.2. – Pl. 14: after El-Sayed & El-Masry, *Athribis* I, pl. VIIIc.

Appendices

Appendix 1: Petrie Museum Archive Negative List

ATHRIBIS & HAGARSEH						
	PMAN	**Description***	**Page in this vol.**	**Excavation Report Ref**	**Bibliographic Ref**	**Museum (Number)**
1.)	591	Athr: '*Athribis. General plan*'	27	Petrie, *Athribis*, pl. XIV	El-Sayed & El-Masry, *Athribis* I, 72, pl. VI	
2.)	592	Athr: '*Athribis. Plan of Temple of* [Ptolemy XII] *Auletes*'	27	Petrie, *Athribis*, pl. XV	El-Sayed & El-Masry, Athribis I, 96, pl. IX	
3.)	593	Athr: '*Athribis. Temple of* [Ptolemy XII] *Auletes. Lintel, trees and Nomes.*' = Lintel above door from room F5 to room L3	36	Petrie, *Athribis*, pl. XIX	El-Sayed & El-Masry, *Athribis* I, 61, 96	
4.)	594	Athr: '*Athribis. Temple of* [Ptolemy XII] *Auletes. Lintel, trees and Nomes.*' = Reliefs in the *soubassement* of room F6, ('Punt chamber') showing incense trees	39	Petrie, *Athribis*, pl. XIX	El-Sayed & El-Masry, *Athribis* I, 88 – Leitz et al., *Aussenwände* I, 245–252	
5.)	595	Athr: '*Athribis. Temple of* [Ptolemy XII] *Auletes. Lintel, trees and Nomes.*' = Reliefs in the *soubassement* of the *couloir mystérieux* (C5) showing nome figures	40	Petrie, *Athribis*, pl. XIX	El-Sayed & El-Masry, *Athribis* I, 229 – Leitz et al. *Athribis* II, 1, 301	
6.)	596	Athr: '*Athribis. Pylon of Physkon. E. face, s. half.*' = Gate of Ptolemy IX, east face, southern door framing	51	Petrie, *Athribis*, pl. XXXII (line drawing)	El-Sayed & El-Masry, *Athribis* I, 152–155	
7.)	597	Athr: '*Athribis. Zodiac tomb. Zodiac A.*'	63	Petrie, *Athribis*, pl. XXXVII		
8.)	598	Athr: '*Athribis. Zodiac tomb. Zodiac B.*'	63	Petrie, *Athribis*, pl. XXXVIII		
9.)	599	Athr: '*Limestone head Ptolemy IX. Athribis.*'	63	Petrie, *Memphis* I, 14, pl. XLV		Manchester (4816)
10.)	600	Athr: '*Limestone head Ptolemy IX. Athribis.*'	63	Petrie, *Memphis* I, 14, pl. XLV		Manchester (4816)
11.)	601	Athr: '*Athribis. Temple of* [Ptolemy XII] *Auletes. Lintel, trees and Nomes.*' = Reliefs in the *soubassement* of room F6, the ('Punt chamber') showing incense trees	39	Petrie, *Athribis*, pl. XIX (line drawing)	El-Sayed & El-Masry, *Athribis* I, 88 – Leitz et al., *Aussenwände* I, 245–252	
12.)	602	Athr: '*Athribis. Temple of* [Ptolemy XII] *Auletes. Outside e. wall.*' = Reliefs on enclosure wall M1	41	Petrie, *Athribis*, pl. XXIII (line drawing)	El-Sayed & El-Masry, *Athribis* I, 96, 125, 126 – Leitz et al., *Aussenwände* I, 67, 72	
13.)	603	Athr: '*Athribis. Temple of* [Ptolemy XII] *Auletes. Outside e. wall.*' = Reliefs on enclosure wall M1	42	Petrie, *Athribis*, pl. XXIV (line drwaing)	El-Sayed & El-Masry, *Athribis* I, 96, 125, 126 – Leitz et al., *Aussenwände* I, 72–73	
14.)	604	Athr: '*Athribis. Temple of* [Ptolemy XII] *Auletes, w. lintel, etc.*' = Reliefs on enclosure wall M3	43	Petrie, *Athribis*, pls. XXVIII, XXIX, XXX (line drawing)		

* Titles of plates reproduced in the excavation reports are given in ''. Authors specifications are given in [].

	PMAN	Description	Page in this vol.	Excavation Report Ref	Bibliographic Ref	Museum (Number)
15.)	605	Athr (?): Limestone stela showing persea (?) tree, offering table and ear (?), attribution questionable	58			?
16.)	606	Athr: 'Roman chapel' (?), reliefs on exterior wall	53	cf. Petrie, *Athribis*, 11, pl. XXXV	El-Sayed & El-Masry, *Athribis* I, 113, 134	
17.)	607	Athr: '*Athribis. Pylon of Physkon. E. face, n. half.*' = Gate of Ptolemy IX, east face, northern door framing	52	Petrie, *Athribis*, pl. XXXI (line drawing)	El-Sayed & El-Masry, *Athribis* I, 158–161	
18.)	608	Athr: Temple of Ptolemy XII, view of the ruined pronaos looking north-east	46		El-Sayed & El-Masry, *Athribis* I, 122	
19.)	609	Athr: Pylon of Ptolemy IX, foundation (?)	50			
20.)	610	Athr: Temple of Ptolemy XII, pronaos, fragmented hathoric capitals and roofing blocks	46		El-Sayed & El-Masry, *Athribis* I, 122	
21.)	611	Athr (?): Temple of Ptolemy XII, fragmented capitals and roofing blocks	47		El-Sayed & El-Masry, *Athribis* I, 122	
22.)	612	Athr: Temple of Ptolemy XII, ambulatory L1 and outer wall M1, view of the excavations looking south	44		El-Sayed & El-Masry, *Athribis* I, 62	
23.)	613	Athr: Temple of Ptolemy IX, view into inner chamber of northern Pylon tower, looking north-east	48	Petrie, *Athribis*, 10–11, pl. XXXV	El-Sayed & El-Masry, *Athribis* I, 87, 135	
24.)	614	Athr: '*Dyers workshop*', view showing vats in the workshop, looking north-west	55	Petrie, *Athribis*, 11, pl. XXXV		
25.)	615	Athr: '*Dyers workshop*', view showing well and cistern in the workshop, looking west	56	Petrie, *Athribis*, 11, pl. XXXV		
26.)	616	Athr: '*Dyers workshop*', view showing cistern and vats in the workshop, looking west	56	Petrie, *Athribis*, 11, pl. XXXV		
27.)	617	Athr (?): Circular stone heap (?)	31			
28.)	618	Athr: Temple of Ptolemy XII, view showing the partly excavated 'Punt Chamber' (F6) and corridor C5, looking south-east	38	Petrie, *Athribis*, pl. XIX	El-Sayed & El-Masry, *Athribis* I, 88	
29.)	619	Athr: West of Temple of Ptolemy XII, view showing workmen at excavation of that temple, looking south	47			
30.)	620	Athr: Temple of Ptolemy XII, enclosure wall M1, view showing partly excavated reliefs and workmen posing	45			
31.)	621	Athr (?): View of rock and pebbles on the mountain, attribution questionable	31			
32.)	622	Athr/Hag: Looking east over the Nile valley from the top of the mountain between Athribis-Atrīpe and al-Hağārisa	30			

	PMAN	Description	Page in this vol.	Excavation Report Ref	Bibliographic Ref	Museum (Number)
33.)	623	Athr/Hag: View of the promontory of Ğabal Adrība near al-Haǧārisa, looking north (?)	28		El-Sayed & El-Masry, *Athribis* I, 80	
34.)	624	Athr: View of the mound with camp set up there, looking south-east	35			
35.)	625	Hag: The „*brick-built deir*" at the foot of the mountain at al-Haǧārisa. Aerial view looking south-east	19	Petrie, *Athribis*, 11, pl. XXXV		
36.)	626	Athr: '*Dyers workshop*', view showing the structure partly refilled with sand, looking north	55	Petrie, *Athribis*, 11, pl. XXV		
37.)	627	Athr: Aerial view of the northern half of the site, looking north-east	33		El-Sayed & El-Masry, *Athribis* I, 79	
38.)	628	Athr: Pylon of Ptolemy IX (?), view of foundations (?)	49			
39.)	629	Athr: View of the western mountain in the northern part of the site	34		El-Sayed & El-Masry, *Athribis* I, 82	
40.)	630	Athr: General view of the mound looking south-east	35		El-Sayed & El-Masry, *Athribis* I, 82	
41.)	631	Hag: General view of the high desert on top of the mountain between al-Haǧārisa and Atrīpe looking west	31			
42.)	632	Athr: Aerial view of the northernmost part of the site, looking north-east	32		El-Sayed & El-Masry, *Athribis* I, 79	
43.)	633	Athr (?): View taken out of one of the tombs in the rock necropolis, looking south-west	29			
44.)	1025	Hag: General view of the site looking west, showing the OK rock necropolis	20	Petrie, *Athribis*, pl. I, line drawing	Kanawati, *El-Hagarsa* I, pl. 1.	
45.)	1026	Hag: „*Tomb of Ka-em-nofer. Plan and sections*"	65	Petrie, *Athribis*, pl. V	Kanawati, *El-Hagarsa* I, 11–20, pls. 3–5, 16–21	
46.)	1027	Hag: „*Tomb of Mery II. N. Wall.*"	22	Petrie, *Athribis*, pl. X	Kanawati, *El-Hagarsa* I, 55–65, pls. 11–15, 41–46	
47.)	1028	Hag: „*Tomb of Mery II. W. Wall.*"	23	Petrie, *Athribis*, pl. XI	Kanawati, *El-Hagarsa* I, 55–65, pls. 11–15, 41–46	
48.)	1029	Hag: „*Tomb of Mery II. S. Wall.*"	24	Petrie, *Athribis*, pl. XII	Kanawati, *El-Hagarsa* I, 55–65, pls. 11–15, 41–46	

Appendix 2: Petrie Museum Archive Negatives Thumbnail Images

ATHRIBIS &
HAGARSEH

PMAN
591 to 633, 1025 to 1029

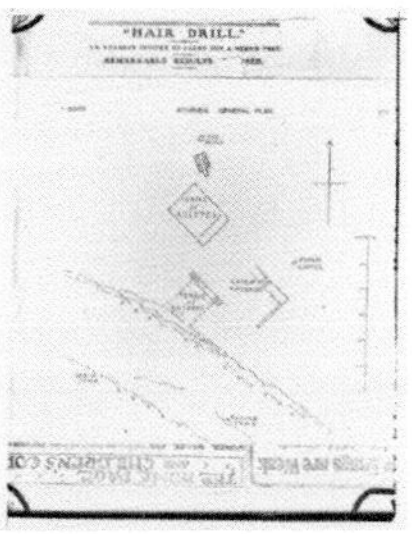
591

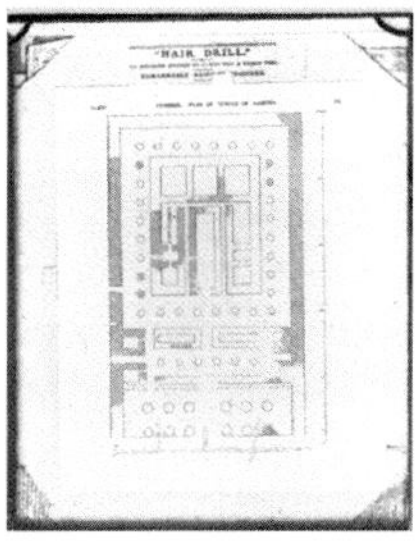
592

593

594

595

596

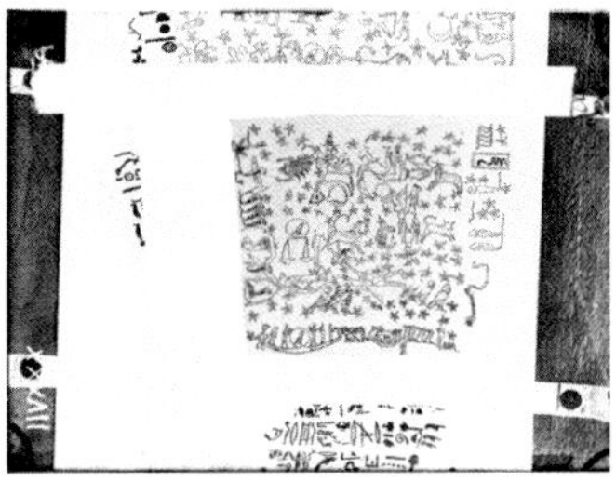
597

598

599

600

601

602

603

604

605

606

607

608

609

610

611

612

613

614

615

616

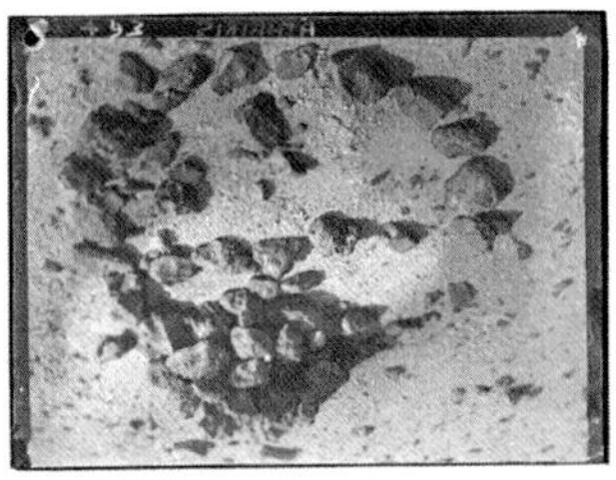
617

618

619

620

621

622

623

624

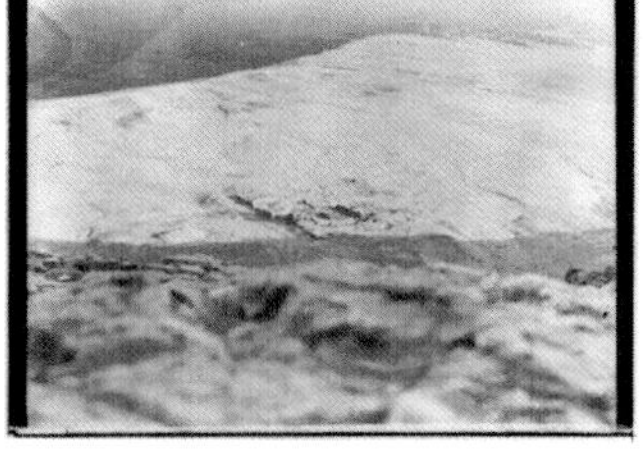
625

626

627

628

629

630

631

632

633

1025

1026

1027

1028

1029

ATHRIBIS &
HAGARSEH

PMAN
591 to 633, 1025 to 1029

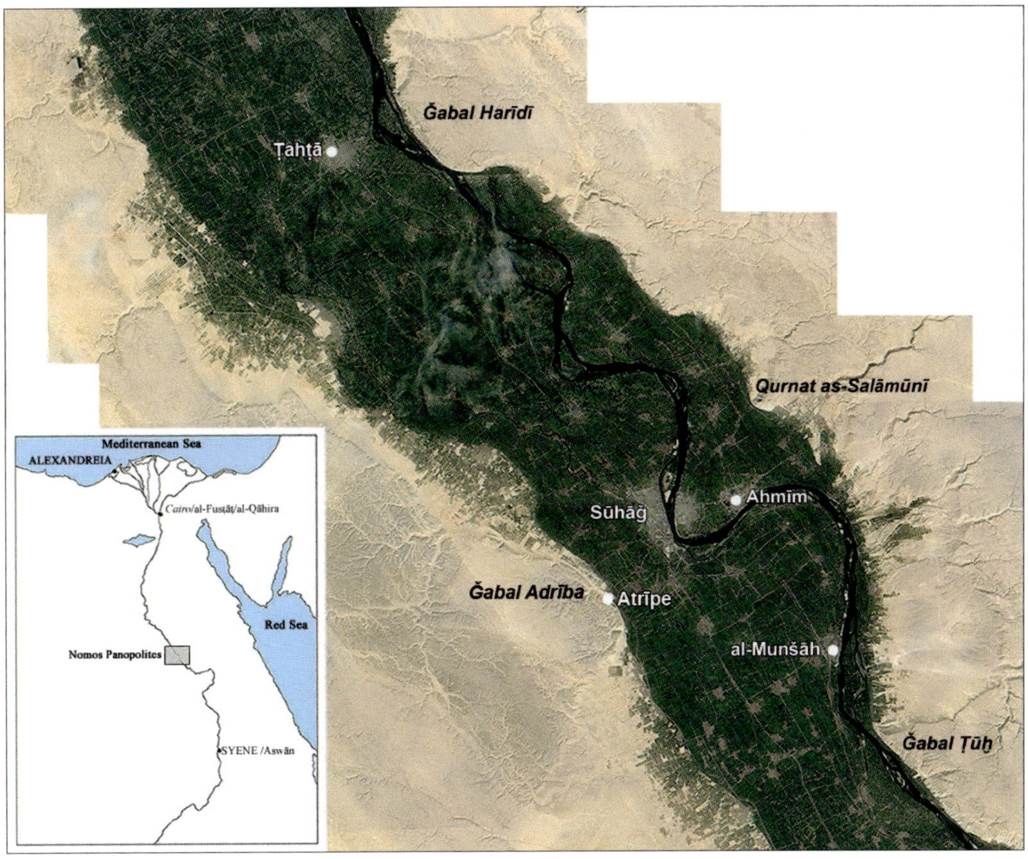

a) Map showing the location of the IXth nome of Upper Egypt and satellite image of the area with toponyms mentioned in the text

b) Satellite image showing the promontory of Mount Atrīpe (west) and the region between Sūhāǧ (north) and al-Kawāmil baḥrī (south) with sites mentioned in the text

Plate II

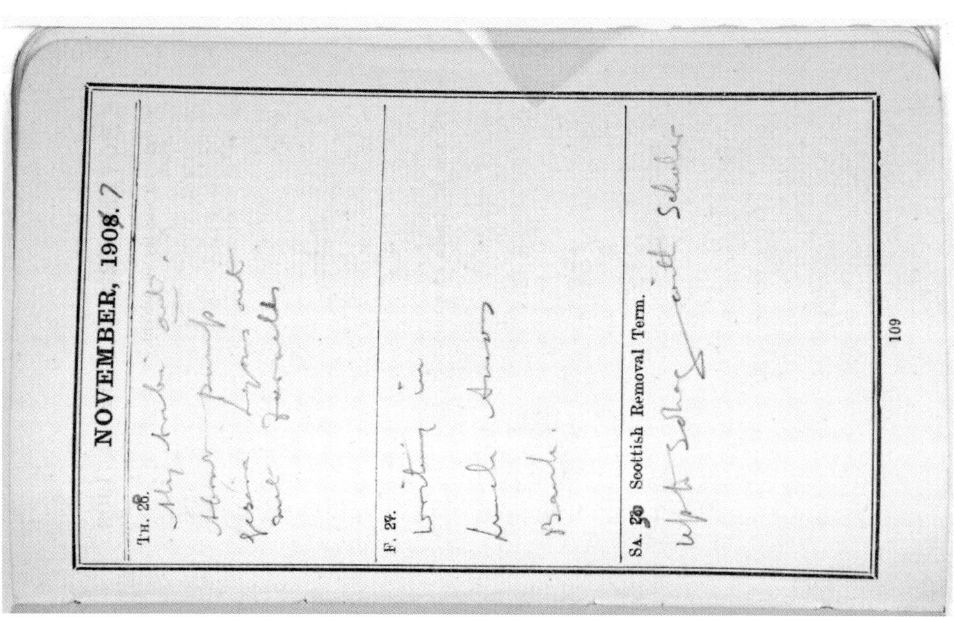

a) Pocket Diary 1907–08, p. 109

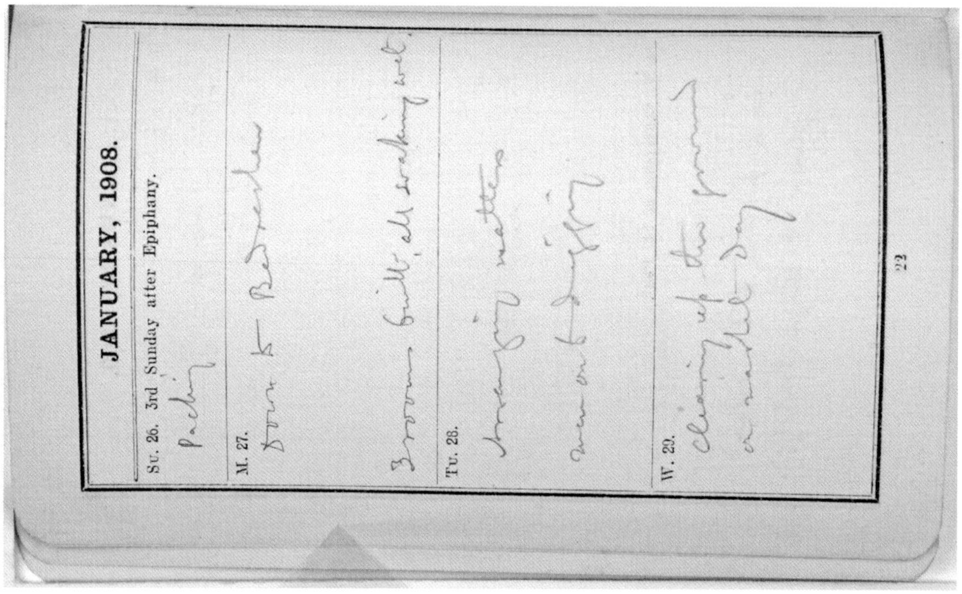

b) Pocket Diary 1907–08, p. 22

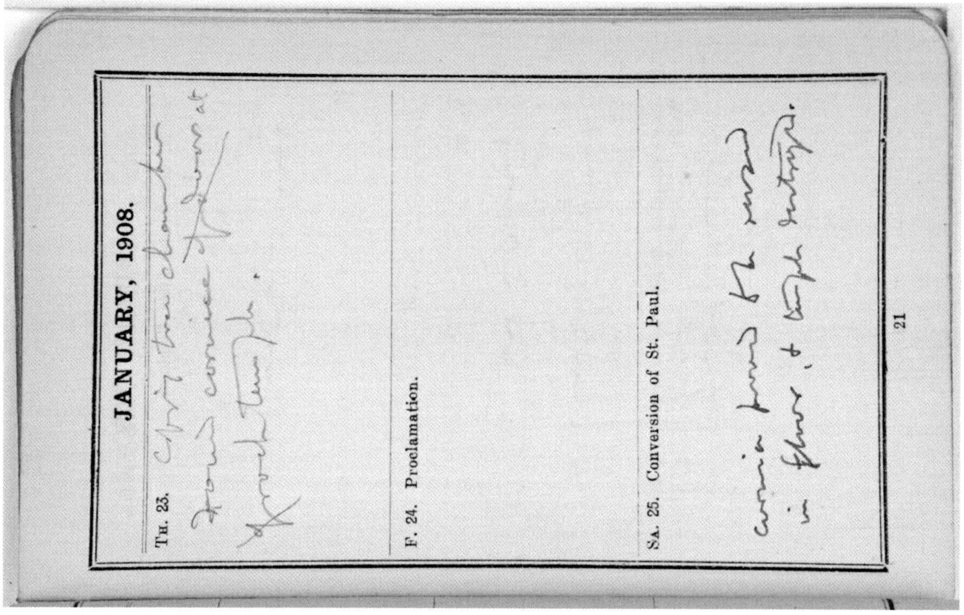

c) Pocket Diary 1907–08, p. 21

a) View of the monumental site of al-Hağārisa (2010)

b) View of the 'monastery' in the plain at the monumental site of al-Hağārisa (2010)

a) View of the Shenute Monastery site (ca 1925)

b) View of the mound at Athribis-Atrīpe, looking east (1983)

a) Athribis-Atrīpe, Temple of Ptolemy XII, lintel of doorway leading from M3 to L3 (1983)

b) Athribis-Atrīpe, Gate of Ptolemy IX, blockage of gateway (1985)

a) View into the Libyan desert plateau at Mount Atrīpe, looking west (2003)

b) Aerial view from the top of the Libyan desert plateau at Mount Atrīpe, looking east (2003)

a) Athribis-Atrīpe, view of the Temple of Ptolemy XII (1983)

b) Athribis-Atrīpe, view of the Pylon of Ptolemy IX (1983)

c) Athribis-Atrīpe, view of the southern part of the site
with remains of 'Roman chapel' [right] (1983)

a) Athribis-Atrīpe, view of the Gate of Ptolemy IX, looking south-east (1983)

b) Athribis-Atrīpe, view of the Gate of Ptolemy IX, looking east (1983)

c) Athribis-Atrīpe, view of the mud brick enclosure wall
south of Temple of Ptolemy IX, looking south-west (1983)

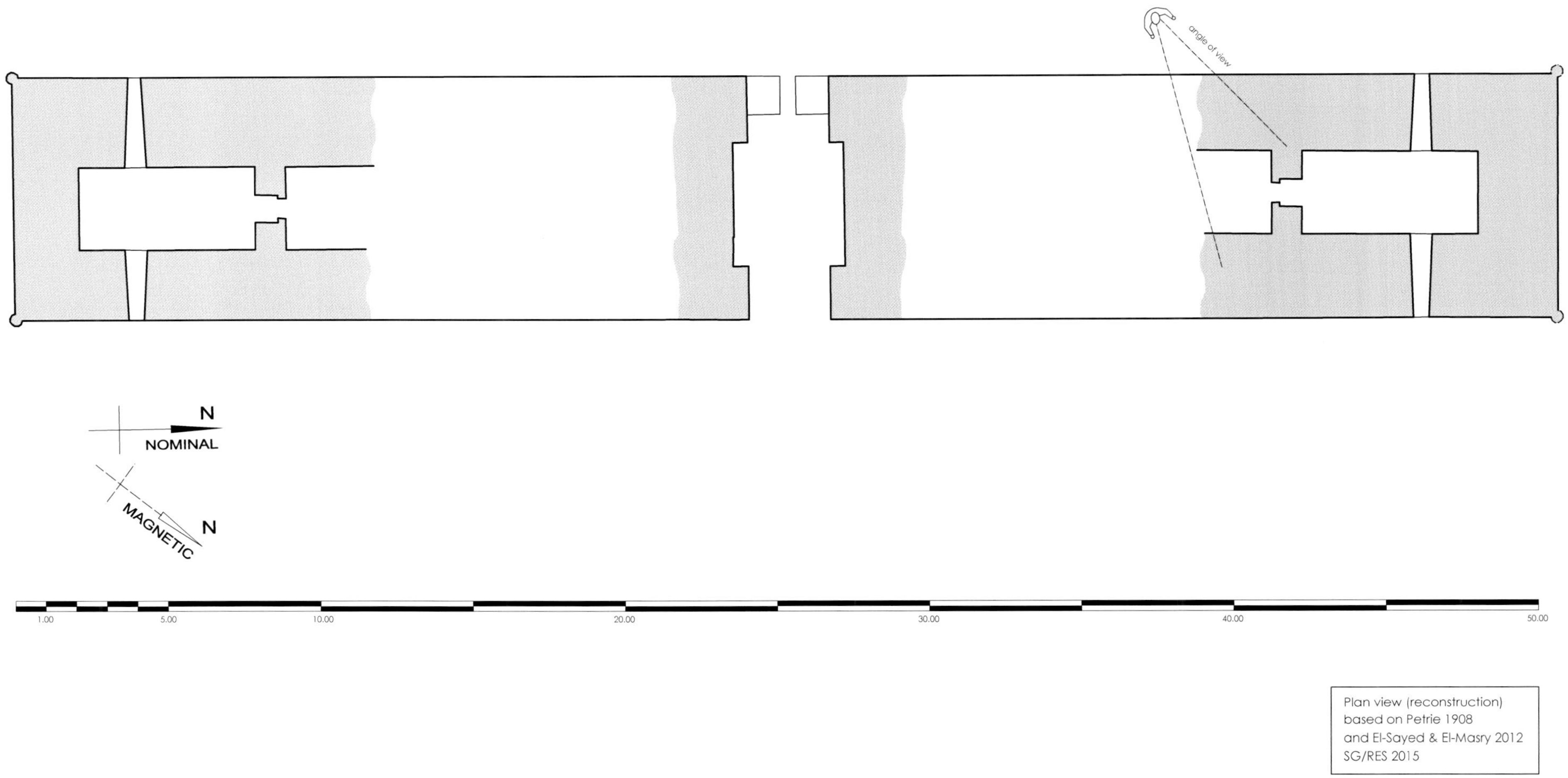

a) Athribis-Atrīpe, Pylon of Temple of Ptolemy IX, plan view (reconstruction based on Petrie, *Athribis*, pl. XXXV and El-Sayed & El-Masry, *Athribis* I, pl. VIII c.

Plate X

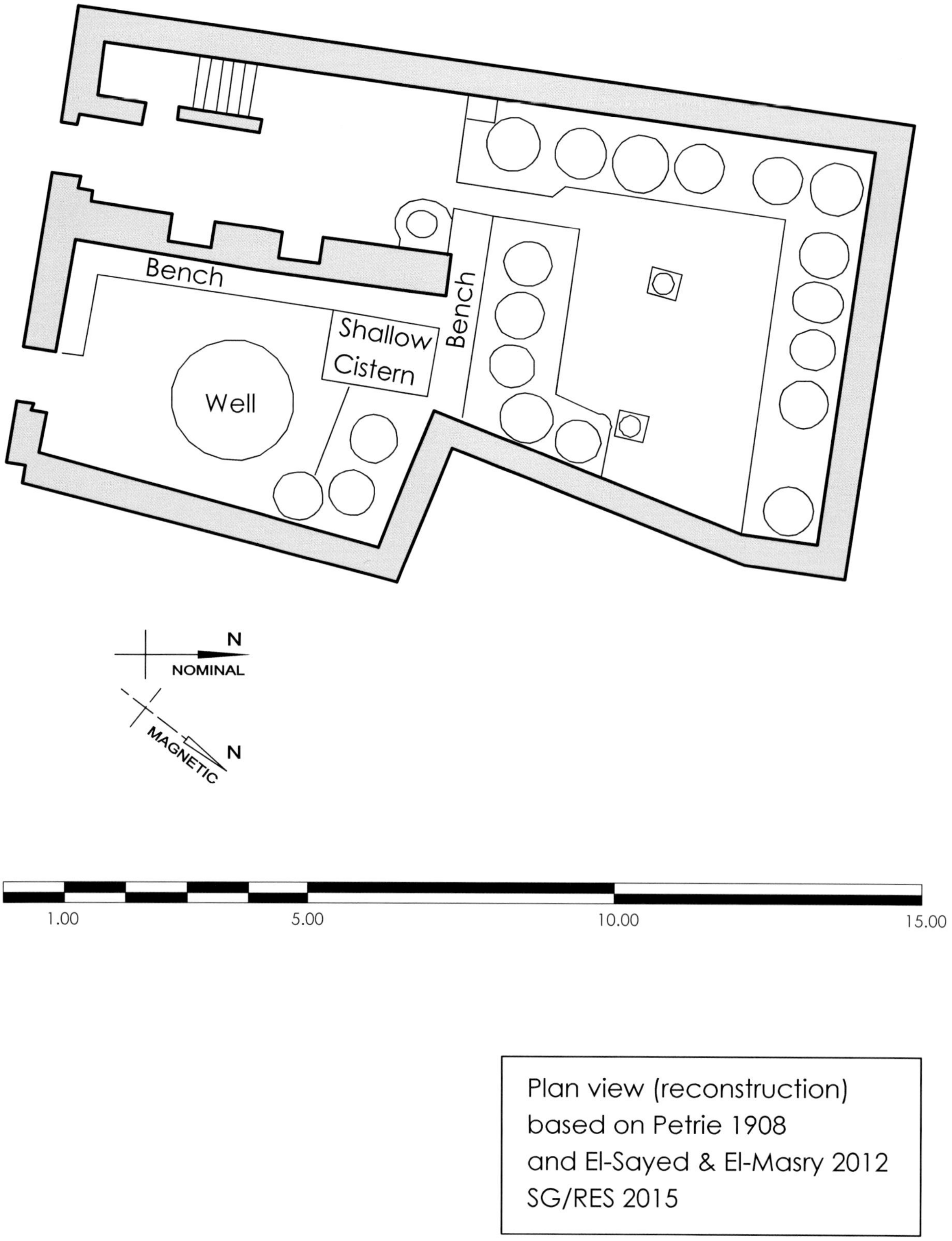

a) Athribis-Atrīpe, Dye works, plan view (reconstruction based on Petrie, *Athribis*, pl. XXXV and El-Sayed & El-Masry, *Athribis* I, pl. VIII c.

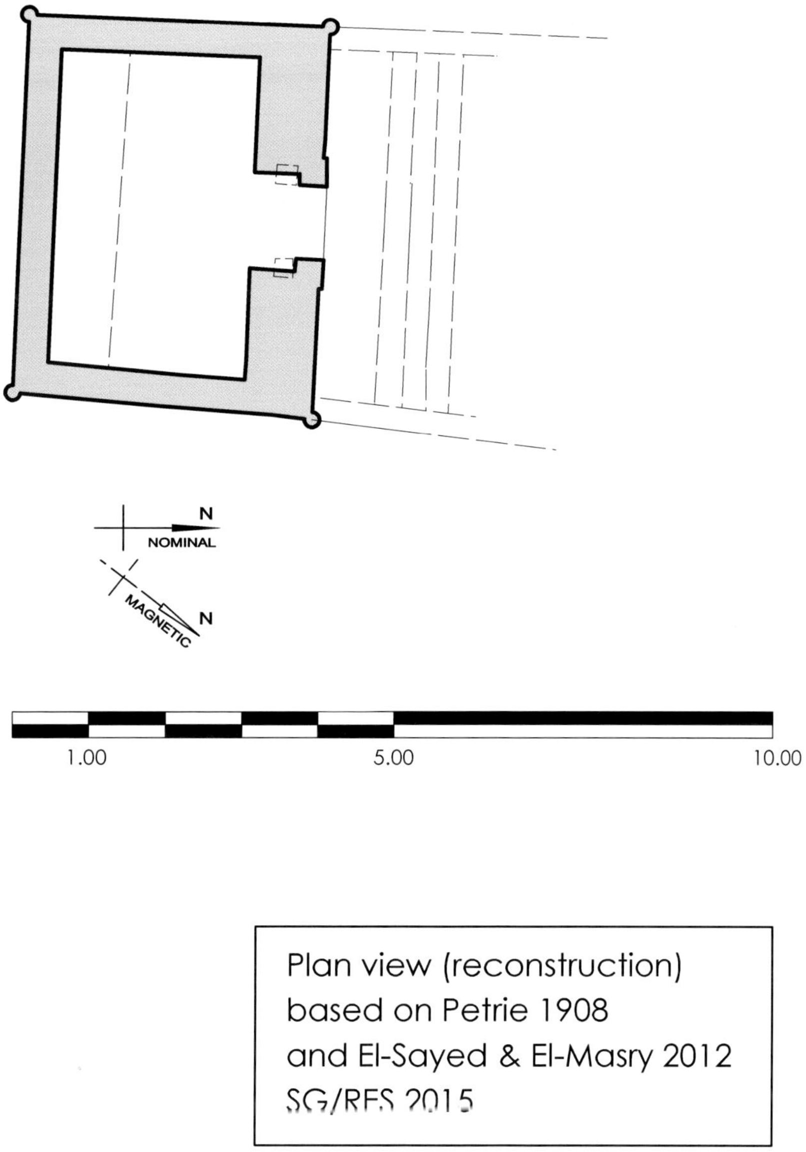

a) Athribis-Atrīpe , 'Roman Chapel', plan view (reconstruction based on Petrie's sketches and the 2003–2011 survey directed by the author)

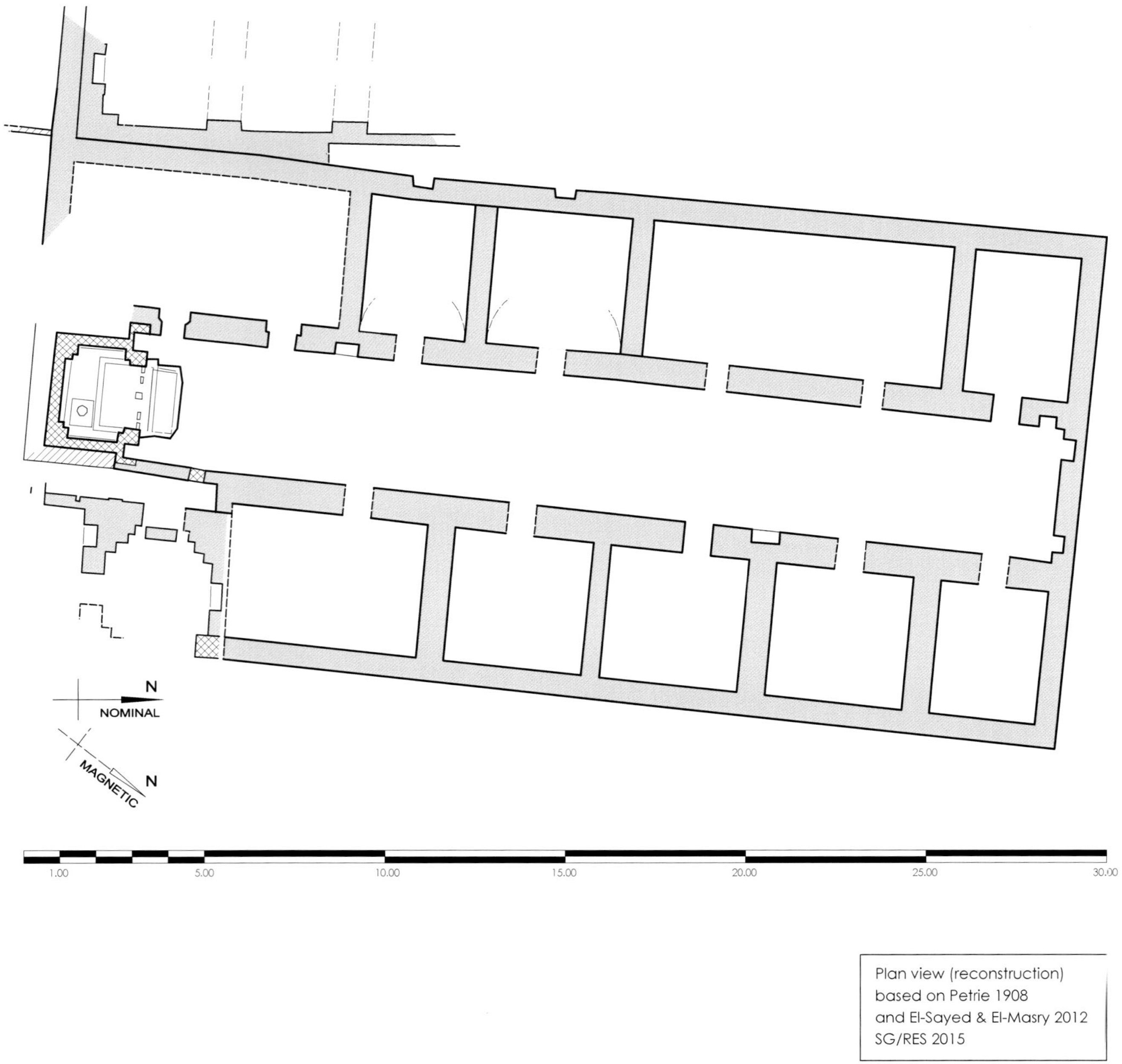

a) Athribis-Atrīpe, ‘monastery’ (infirmery [?]), plan view (reconstruction based on Petrie’s sketches and the 2003–2011 survey directed by the author)

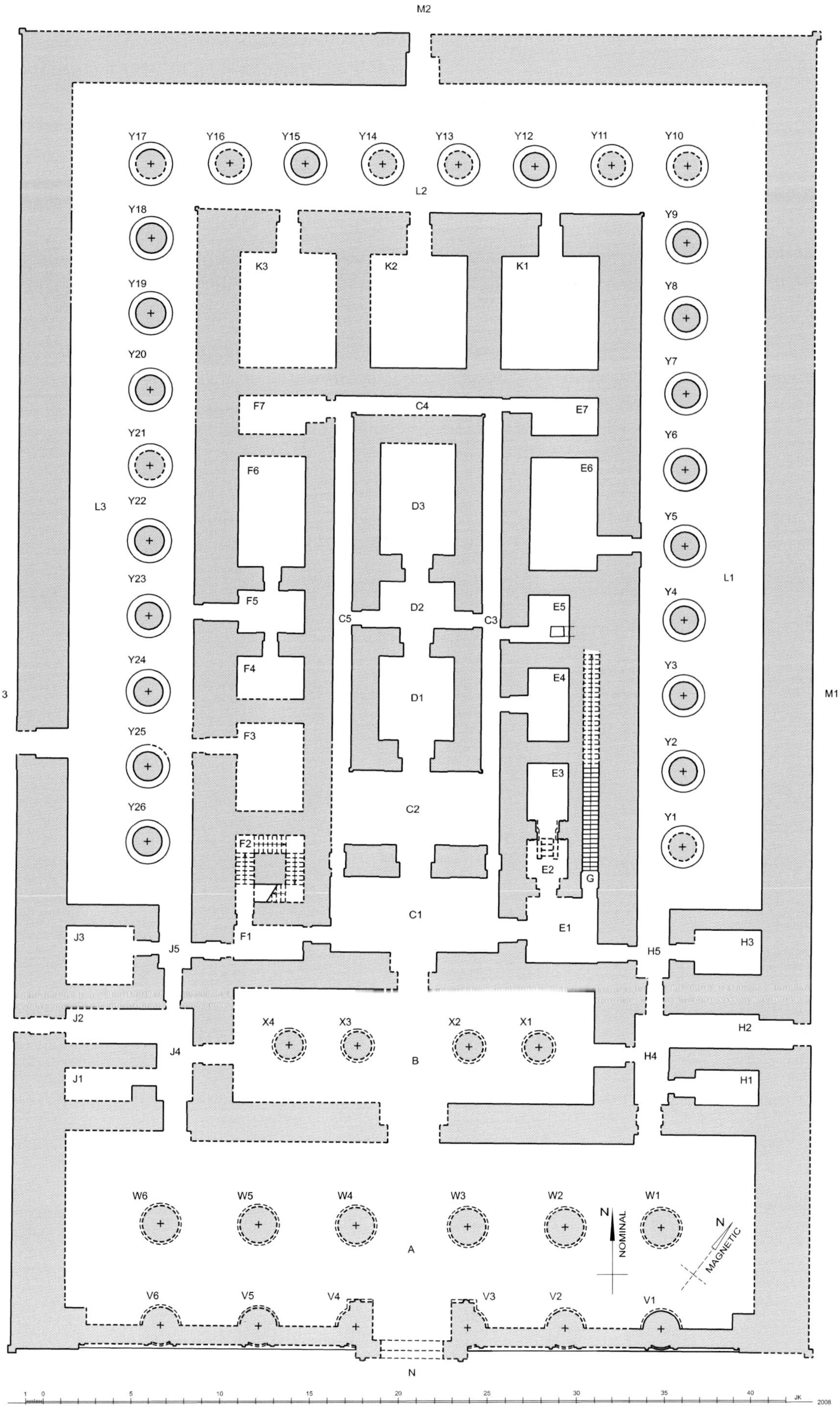

a) Plan of the Temple of Ptolemy XII at Athribis-Atrīpe (after El-Sayed & El-Masry, *Athribis* I, 96 [fig. 2.2.2.])

Plate XIV

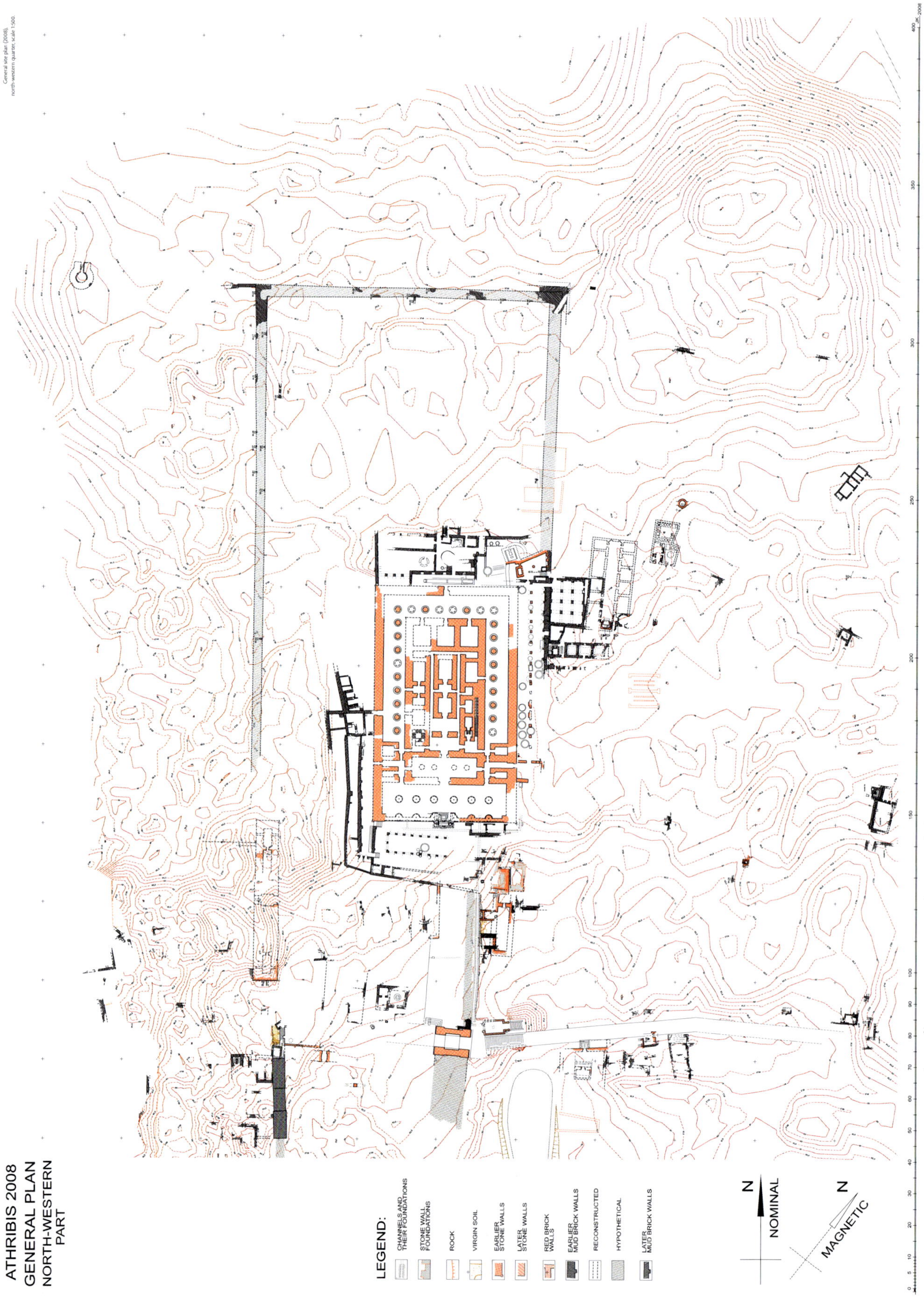

b) Athribis-Antrīpe, general plan, north-eastern part of the site, after El-Sayed & El-Masry, *Athribis* I, pl. VIIIc